Synthesis Lectures on Information Concepts, Retrieval, and Services

Series Editor

Gary Marchionini, School of Information and Library Science, The University of North Carolina at Chapel Hill, Chapel Hill, NC, USA

This series publishes short books on topics pertaining to information science and applications of technology to information discovery, production, distribution, and management. Potential topics include: data models, indexing theory and algorithms, classification, information architecture, information economics, privacy and identity, scholarly communication, bibliometrics and webometrics, personal information management, human information behavior, digital libraries, archives and preservation, cultural informatics, information retrieval evaluation, data fusion, relevance feedback, recommendation systems, question answering, natural language processing for retrieval, text summarization, multimedia retrieval, multilingual retrieval, and exploratory search.

Rhiannon Bettivia · Yi-Yun Cheng ·
Michael Robert Gryk

Documenting the Future: Navigating Provenance Metadata Standards

Rhiannon Bettivia
Boston, MA, USA

Michael Robert Gryk
Farmington, CT, USA

Yi-Yun Cheng
New Brunswick, NJ, USA

ISSN 1947-945X   ISSN 1947-9468   (electronic)
Synthesis Lectures on Information Concepts, Retrieval, and Services
ISBN 978-3-031-18702-5   ISBN 978-3-031-18700-1   (eBook)
https://doi.org/10.1007/978-3-031-18700-1

This Springer imprint is published by the registered company Springer Nature Switzerland AG
The registered company address is: Gewerbestrasse 11, 6330 Cham, Switzerland

RB would like to dedicate her contributions in this book to her family.
YYC would like to dedicate her contributions to her family and friends.
MRG would like to dedicate his contributions to the Locke family in thanks for loaning him the Echo key.

Preface

It is fitting that a book on provenance should begin by talking about its own origins. The origins of our collaboration began when we were colleagues at the University of Illinois, School of Information Sciences circa 2016–2018. At the iSchool, we worked on various aspects of provenance in our multiple roles as students, researchers, educators and scholars. Irrespective of the setting, one deceptively simple question always arose: why use PREMIS rather than PROV and vice versa?

The question is one of those questions that seems simple, while in reality it hides a multitude of flexible and changeable answers. It is like asking why someone chose an Apple computer over a Windows computer. Some responses will refer to the performance of the architecture, the software that is included or a perceived ease-of-use. Yet in the end, the true, heartfelt answer often comes down to a simple preference: *I like Apple* or *I like Windows*. That type of answer is not satisfying when considering a metadata standard. It doesn't seem sufficient to say one *likes* PROV or one *likes* ProvONE or one *likes* PREMIS. We are driven towards a more objective, professional response. This book is the latest step in a long journey we have made in addressing questions about how one chooses to structure provenance and why.

We will perhaps date ourselves at some point in the future when we say that this project began in earnest in the before times of the COVID-19 pandemic. As it was, we organized a workshop on provenance metadata for the 15th International Digital Curation Conference, held in Dublin, Ireland, on February 17, 2020. The workshop was entitled *Navigating through the Panoply of Provenance: Metadata Standards useful for Digital Curation*, and its goal was to help educate practitioners about these three metadata standards, PROV, ProvONE and PREMIS, along with their pros and cons for various purposes. The first half of the workshop covered the three standards along with exercises on their use. The second half of the workshop was a hands-on session in which the participants were tasked with creating a provenance record for a topic. The participants were split into separate groups such that one group used PROV while another used PREMIS to tackle the same underlying data. Once complete, the groups then swapped metadata records and attempted to crosswalk between PROV and PREMIS. We had a delightful time discussing provenance standards, crosswalking metadata by hand, and of course, sipping Irish

Fig. 1 Photos of workshop activity at IDCC 2020, Dublin, Ireland

stouts. It was also, unbeknownst to us at the time, the last of our in-person professional engagements for a couple of years (Fig. 1).

The workshop was a success, and much was learned by the participants as well as by us. The biggest revelation from the participants was a renewed sense of confidence in tackling provenance issues at their home institutions. Documenting provenance in a digital world means working in technologically complex environments, even when the objects in question are analog. Participants stated that, after the workshop, they were ready to try to implement standardized approaches or to mediate more fruitful conversations between content specialists and IT infrastructure personnel.

Additional workshops were included in the programs for the 83rd ASIS&T Annual Meeting and at iConference 2021. Our second workshop happened in March 2021, when working-from-home had become the new norm. Despite the lack of face-to-face connections, we could still interact in real time on our colorful online whiteboard, made specifically for the online conference experience. The virtual environment crafted inside a Miro Board enabled us to use the video game *Animal Crossing: New Horizons* to help

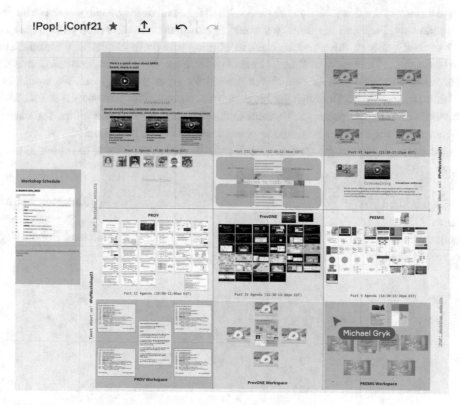

Fig. 2 Photo of workshop activity at iConference 2020, online

explore provenance and *¡PoP!*, a panoply of provenance metadata standards, with some much needed cuteness and cheer during dark times (Fig. 2).

This book is the latest step on our journey, one where we hope to share what we've learned along the way with a larger audience. The Oxford English Dictionary defines the word "provenance" as origin, source, ownership of an artwork or guidance to determine authenticity. Provenance, as we know it today, is not limited to history domains. It has many faces in different fields: phylogeny concerns the tree of life of species; genealogy studies the ancestry of families; stratigraphy dates layers of sediments. The idea of provenance transcends disciplines, and this book *Documenting the Future: Navigating Provenance Metadata Standards* is intended for anyone in any field who has a keen spirit to dabble in the world of provenance. Perhaps echoing life in general, provenance is more about the journey than the destination. We don't claim to have an authoritative answer to that deceptively simple question of why we choose one provenance standard over another. Our hope is that the chapters in this book will help empower the reader to frame and answer provenance questions on their own.

We did not make this journey alone and wish to thank all of the people who have helped along the way. First and foremost, we would like to thank our workshop participants for their curiosity, energy, drive and feedback in working with these standards. We would also like to thank the University of Illinois, School of Information Sciences, and the Center for Informatics Research in Science and Scholarship for all of their support. We would like to thank Dr. Jerome McDonough for his comments on modeling provenance in PREMIS. We would also like to thank Dr. Bertram Ludäscher and Dr. Tim McPhillips for sharing their expertise regarding provenance in general and this book in particular.

Last and certainly not the least, we thank you, the reader, for joining us on our journey. Enjoy.

Massachusetts, USA   Rhiannon Bettivia
Illinois, USA   Yi-Yun Cheng
Connecticut, USA   Michael Robert Gryk
December 2022

Contents

At the Intersection of Provenance and Metadata

The paintings represented in Fig. 1.1 are by artists Claude Monet and Winslow Homer. Both paintings featured in the BBC's popular television program, *Fake or Fortune*[1] in which reporter Fiona Bruce and art dealer Philip Mould examine the provenance of 'sleepers', or an artwork of dubious origin. Through forensic study of the paintings' materials and their historical traces, the show attempts to determine whether each item is worth a fortune or is a fake. The Monet painting was found to be genuine by the show's researchers: its style, pigments, and history suggested the work was genuine. However, the non-profit foundation that manages the artist's legacy refused to accept the show's findings and declined to include the painting in a *catalogue raisonné* (a comprehensive and annotated list of all known works by an artist), functionally rendering the artwork fake in the eyes of buyers. Works not included in an artist's *catalogue raisonné* are not considered to be legitimate. The second painting, by artist Winslow Homer, was shown to be real after someone discovered it in a dumpster and brought it to an open session for the UK television show *Antiques Roadshow*. The painting became embroiled in a multi-year ownership dispute when the owners of the house from which the paintings were thrown away exerted their ownership claim over the rights of the person who found the painting in the garbage (Fig. 1.1).

The idea of provenance is not new. The ability to tell the story of objects stretches back hundreds, if not thousands, of years. In some industries, provenance is bread and butter. In the two cases above, literal fortunes are gained or lost through provenance. *Fake or Fortune* demonstrates time and again that physical, chemical, and stylistic analysis alone cannot determine the authenticity of an historical object: authenticity is not inherent, physical properties. Forgers use repurposed materials, ancient techniques, and careful stylistic recreation to create fake works of art. In such cases, it is the unbroken chain of history, the provenance, that can trace the object from the creator's hand to the present moment that serves as the ironclad proof of authenticity.

---

[1] BBC's *Fake or Fortune*: https://www.bbc.co.uk/programmes/b01mxxz6.

R. Bettivia et al., *Documenting the Future: Navigating Provenance Metadata Standards*, Synthesis Lectures on Information Concepts, Retrieval, and Services, https://doi.org/10.1007/978-3-031-18700-1_1

Fig. 1.1 Left: a Claude Monet; Right: a Winslow Homer

1.1   Metadata

Given the importance of provenance, it is no wonder that so many domain spaces devote standards and community practices to documenting it. One way to keep track of provenance is via some kind of *metadata* standard. Metadata literally means *data about data*. In practice, we need more functional ways to talk about what metadata making and metadata using look like. Archivist Anne Gilliland defines metadata as, "...the sum total of what one can say at a given moment about any information object at any level of aggregation" [1]. Jane Greenberg, Director of the Metadata Research Center at Drexel University, describes metadata as, "...structured data about an object that supports functions associated with the designated object" [2]. The National Information Standards Organization (NISO) Primer on metadata says simply that "[metadata is] structured information with elements and properties" [3]. The variety of definitions in use stems in part from the fact that metadata is everywhere, used and created by people everyday. In information science, we tend to think about metadata in the realm of professionals: data managers or library catalogers making validating records in JSON or XML. But metadata work is now the daily province of many non-professionals. Some readers may be old enough to remember the days of copying songs from a CD onto a computer and having to enter track titles and artist information by hand: this is metadata making. We currently live in a world of metadata exhaust [4], where much of our quotidian digital interactions create metadata that leave provenance traces behind: whenever we send a Tweet or participate in a Zoom meeting, metadata about user names involved, IP addresses and GIS coordinates, duration and timestamps, chats and Tweet text, etc. are generated and collected.

Metadata comes in all shapes, sizes, and flavors. Jenn Riley's germinal 2009 *Seeing Standards* visualization encompasses a rainbow of options, breaking down some existing schemas by domain, community, function and purpose [5]. The landscape has inarguably grown in the time since. Provenance metadata is one of many, non-canonical forms of metadata. True, mutually exclusive categorizations of metadata are elusive, given the shifting nature of data: the same information can be data, metadata, paradata, content surrogates, or information objects, depending on context. What is technical metadata can also aid in administration; what is preservation metadata can also rely on description. Some of the many categories of metadata include:

- Descriptive
- Technical
- Structural
- Rights
- Administrative
- Preservation
- Use
- Meta-metadata
- Contextual
- Aboutness of users
- And, of course, provenance.

The complexity of categorizing metadata is further compounded by its sheer ubiquity: it is used in commercial spaces as much as research, academic, and public sector domains. Each discipline and industry has its own schemas and attendant controlled vocabularies, rules of description, and both *de facto* and *de jure* norms of creation and use.

Provenance metadata exemplifies the challenges of general metadata categorization. The history of an object–how it was made and what its features are–might feature aspects of descriptive, technical, use, and structural metadata. Its history of ownership and travels through the world might be reflected in administrative and rights metadata. Provenance information refers to the history, the ownership, and the origins of an object. In a digital context, this definition includes process and other contextual information. Provenance requires some basic descriptive metadata in the need to provide benchmarks that help identify the object and thus ensure, over time, that the object maintains its essential characteristics. These essential characteristics are sometimes called *significant properties*. Provenance is also sometimes seen as a subset of administrative metadata. Administrative metadata is metadata that helps in the care and maintenance of an object; it is data for the stewards of objects to help them in their job of stewardship. Provenance fits under this general category because its ability to tell a story about where the object has been helps stewards to make decisions about where the object should go. Provenance also shares a good deal of overlap with preservation metadata, or data that fills the role of providing information regarding previous conservation activities and to inform future preservation choices for an object. Preservation metadata should, minimally, uniquely identify the object in question; describe a functional technological environment for the object; and track preservation activities. It should also detail the history, ownership, origins, process, and context for an object. Finally, preservation metadata lays out the processes that will be taken in the future to maintain access to objects. In other words, it represents the full temporal spectrum of provenance. Provenance is the weaving together of metadata items to tell a cohesive story about an object. The story is a persuasive one: it either successfully establishes the object as what it purports to be, or it fails to convince. The self-same chain of provenance might convince some audiences and not others, as evidenced by *Fake or Fortune* episodes wherein experts disagree, such as the case of the Monet at the outset of this chapter.

1.2 Provenance

Provenance does not only pertain to works in museums, galleries, and archives, like the paintings at the beginning of this book. It is perhaps telling that most of the articles about the television show *Fake or Fortune* focus on property and other legal concerns [6, 7]. In the realm of digital content, the ability to create endless perfect copies of an original work complicates notions of originality, authenticity, and integrity. A physical painting, like the Winslow Homer above, can only be in one location at any given time and therefore can be followed on a singular path over time if you have a lot of good record keeping and a bit of luck: from painter, to house, to dumpster. A digital file, on the other hand, can exist simultaneously in many places at once. When Bettivia writes a draft chapter of this book and shares it with Cheng by sending a Word document via email, identical copies exist on Bettivia's computer and Cheng's computer, along with any copies floating around the servers of the email providers. While the content of the documents themselves may be identical such that a message digest, like an MD5 or SHA checksum, for each one is the same, their location on different machines–Bettivia's computer, Cheng's computer, the email provider's server– marks the copies as fundamentally different. They appear on different hardware, different software versions for different operating systems, different disc sectors, and in relation to different materials.

For digital objects, the custodial chain and change logs establish their trustworthiness and realness. Yet measurable properties or even questions about the identity of digital objects are distinct from analog objects, and the complexity of computational products and processes require a different method of recording and reporting their provenance. Further, modeling provenance and recording different stages of a research project, especially in the context of collaborative data science, computational science, and other eScience domains presents their own challenges. The lack of provenance metadata for born-digital objects in each stage of a research pipeline can reduce the transparency, trustworthiness, and reproducibility of collaborative projects. In computational research, the process of doing the work often yields as much or more information than the analysis alone, requiring formalized standards for documenting scientific workflows. Xu et al. [8] state that reliance on process in the area of computer supported collaborative work has actually changed and expanded traditional uses of the term provenance beyond the way it has been applied in disciplines like art history [8]:

The notion of provenance has been adopted and extended in the field of Computer Science and applied to concepts such as data, computation, user interaction, and reasoning. In this context, provenance is no longer limited to origin or history, but also includes the process and other contextual information.

What provenance means in a rapidly digitizing world is evolving, as it comes to incorporate aspects of process documentation, workflows, and reproducibility documentation. The documentation of workflows can be seen as part of larger conversations about visualizing processes as provenance. Metadata is both ubiquitous and necessary; in the information age, the sheer volume and diversity of digital objects requires metadata as a navigational aid. Contextualization via provenance metadata may help to improve speed and accuracy when drawing new conclusions from previous work [9]. Sensemaking and other research that relies on crowdsourcing also relies on provenance metadata in order to understand and legitimize the outcomes [10]. Further, provenance metadata is essential in establishing trust when new technologies, like blockchain for example, enter common use in long-established fields, such as arts and archives [11, 12]. As fields like these reckon with the disruption of inventions like non-fungible tokens (NFTs), the contextualization of provenance is part of what allays concerns about deep fakes and fears about the ways in which repurposed artifacts may impede the ability of archival materials to accurately represent historical records [13].

Tracking the movement of objects over a single computational research project is a challenge. Provenance in such cases is ultimately a tool designed to help manage futures that have yet to materialize: it addresses what could be in addition to what is and what has been. With art, that challenge extends to many human lifetimes and we are often left picking up threads that have been left hanging for years. In those cases, we are reconstructing the past. Either way, provenance is challenging because it is often an exercise in documentational time travel. Formal documentation schemas enable us to create descriptive chains both forward and backward in time: provenance chains echo from the past into the future. Standardization allows us to share provenance with others. In this textbook, we consider three existing models for documenting provenance. In introducing these provenance models, we address overarching concerns such as:

- Where does provenance happen?
- What provenance can be modeled and documented before something happens (traces of the past), what must be done during (processes, crowdsourcing), and after (workflows and plans)?

This book will take up these questions. It combines basic introductions to provenance standards with mini-exercises, all with the aim to inspire readers to think about what provenance means in their institutions and their work.

1.3   How This Book Works

Provenance is ubiquitous in the study of information. It is an old and established idea: in 1440, Lorenzo Valla wrote *Declamatio de falso dredita et ementita donatione Constantini*, his "Discourse on the Forgery of the Alleged Donation of Constantine". Within the digital realm broadly, provenance takes on additional complexity as the ease of duplication, speed of obsolescence, and rise of computational research challenge our traditionally analog notions and practices of documenting process, authenticity, and integrity. Different domain spaces have different uses for provenance metadata, ranging from preservation to version control to workflow standardization and documentation for research. The focus of this book is the documentation of provenance and the role it plays in digital research and productions.

We start by offering a simple, unifying definition of provenance for purposes of this book: provenance is a description of how something comes to be. We explore some representative established standards for documenting provenance: *PREMIS*, *PROV*, and *ProvONE*. **PREMIS** is an international metadata standard developed by an Editorial Committee and hosted by the US Library of Congress to support digital preservation and curation. **PROV** is a family of models and standards proposed by the W3C. It is used to document provenance information about data and digital objects. **ProvONE** is a PROV extension which includes concepts and attributes for specifying workflows and data products produced by their execution, particularly in eScience disciplines. Despite domain differences, these provenance metadata models retain some similar key features, such as their top-level entities, particularly agents and events. Here, we present the foundations of these provenance standards, a deep exploration of each one, and examples of their use in professional practice.

As we discuss and evaluate each standard, emphasis will be placed on highlighting the strengths and capabilities of each model, as well as shortcomings of any individual model which are better handled by one or more of the others. The aim of the mini-exercises is not necessarily to make a corpus of validating records using these schemas, but rather to understand the entities and perspectives these standards represent in order to inform processes relevant to readers' work. While these schemas were designed for very specific tasks, they have the flexibility to encompass sensemaking, process documentation, and the broad range of data that falls under the provenance big tent.

In Chap. 2, we introduce the PROV family of standards and key ideas and concepts relating to PROV. The chapter describes PROV and scenarios in which a reader might use it. We introduce the core components in PROV, *entities*, *activities*, and *agents*, and we create simple diagrams and Python snippets using simplified wine making processes as an example.

Chapter 3 introduces more advanced concepts in PROV. We cover relationships between core concepts including generalization, usage, and derivations. Following the wine example from vat to special fermentation process to bottle, the chapter explores the PROV mechanisms of alternates and specializations that allow us to describe the same entities at different levels of abstraction. Bundles and plans lead to the introduction of the concepts of provenance of provenance and of prospective provenance, provenance of what can and/or will be in future.

In Chap. 4, we examine the related standard, ProvONE. ProvONE was designed with a specific focus on eScience workflows. The ProvONE model aims to bridge *retrospective provenance* (traces) and *prospective provenance* (workflows): documenting the relationships between what has already happened with what might happen in the future. The mini-exercise builds a domain-non-specific example on the process of creating content in the popular simulation video game, Nintendo's *Animal Crossing: New Horizons*.

Chapter 5 steers away from the W3C PROV family and introduces the digital preservation metadata standard, PREMIS. It covers PREMIS basics including its creation and its version history up until its current iteration, version 3.0. PREMIS was designed to mirror the dominant standard in digital preservation, the Open Archival Information System (OAIS). In recent years, it has made moves towards compatibility with Semantic Web environments with an OWL-ontology and a less linear information model. This chapter explores the four main functional entities in a PREMIS record and the ways in which version 3.0 describes relationships between entities.

Chapter 6, Advanced PREMIS, covers topics such as object relationships and environments. It also stretches PREMIS beyond digital preservation to cover provenance more generally, exploring the use of controlled vocabulary terms and user-generated terms with PREMIS events as part of a mini-exercise documenting software version updates of *Animal Crossing: New Horizons*.

In much the same way that ProvONE extends PROV beyond its original boundaries to address the full temporal spectrum of provenance, Chap. 7 takes PREMIS beyond its home in digital preservation. We explore a real-world application of PREMIS in the domain of nuclear magnetic resonance (NMR) spectroscopy using a tool called Workflow Builder. In contrast to previous chapters where we start with retrospective provenance (past events) and work towards prospective provenance (future events), Chap. 7 examines a situation wherein scientists struggled to document retrospective provenance that happens quickly in a computational environment. Prior to the work described in Chap. 7, scientists in the NMR spectroscopy domain were reliant on using prospective workflow documentation as a surrogate for modeling which steps and algorithms were actually used in past experiments and transformations. Customized uses of PREMIS enable spectroscopists to document both what has happened and what workflows they might employ in the future.

In our concluding chapter, Chap. 8, we discuss PROV, ProvONE, and PREMIS altogether by taking the readers through some real-world applications and barriers of these models. We then discuss some lingering issues concerning appraisal, circularity, and cross-walking with provenance models that are still unresolved at this point in time. We conclude this book with a call for action to the readers to write your own provenance stories.

1.4   Summary

For those working with digital data, this book presents an introduction to provenance standards with the hope that readers will be able to build on this research as they develop their own practice in documenting processes and origins, how things come to be. Each chapter introduces the basic know-hows of the model, with explorations on more advanced edge cases in later sections. Each chapter concludes with simple mini-exercises in which the standards are brought into conversation with real-world data.

Case studies and examples cover the creation of basic records using a variety of provenance metadata models; proper use of provenance relations to connect the entities; and the differences between PROV, ProvONE, and PREMIS. Readers can be expected to gain an understanding of the uses of provenance metadata and data models in different domains in order to make informed decisions on their use. Documenting provenance can be a daunting challenge and it is hoped that with these clear examples and explanations, the task will be less intimidating and readers will have a foothold to begin tackling their own provenance needs.

References

1. Baca M (2016) Introduction to metadata. Getty Research Institute, Los Angeles
2. Greenberg J (2005) Understanding metadata and metadata schemes. Cat Classification Q 40:17–36
3. Riley J (2017) Understanding metadata. National Information Standards Organization. http://niso.org/publications/press/UnderstandingMetadata.pdf. Cited 10 Mar 2022
4. Pomerantz J (2015) Metadata. MIT Press, Cambridge
5. Riley J (2009) Seeing standards: a visualization of the metadata universe. http://jennriley.com/metadatamap/seeingstandards.pdf. Cited 10 Mar 2022
6. Bandle AL (2015) Fake or fortune? art authentication rules in the art market and at court. Int J Cult Prop 22:379–399
7. Herman A (2014) The fake chagall, the asphalt jungle and moral rights in france. Art Antiquity & Law, United Kingdom
8. Xu K, Ottley A, Walchshofer C, Streit M, Chang R, Wenskovitch J (2020) Survey on the analysis of user interactions and visualization provenance. Comput Graph Forum 38(3):757–783
9. Sarvghad A, Tory M (2015) Exploiting analysis history to support collaborative data analysis. In: Proceedings of the 41st graphics interface conference. Canadian Information Processing Society, Canada
10. Wiggins A, He Y (2016) Community-based data validation practices in citizen science. In: Proceedings of the 19th ACM conference on computer supported cooperative work and social computing. Association for Computing Machinery, pp 1548–1559

11. Dell N, Perrier T, Kumar N, Lee M, Powers R, Borriello G (2015) Digital workflows in global development organizations. In: Proceedings of the 18th ACM conference on computer supported cooperative work and social computing. Association for Computing Machinery, pp 1659–1669
12. Woodall A, Ringel S (2020) Blockchain archival discourse: trust and the imaginaries of digital preservation. New Media Soc 22(12):2200–2217
13. Prelinger R (2021) NFTs and AI are unsettling the very concept of history. https://www.wired.com/story/nfts-and-ai-are-unsettling-the-very-concept-of-history. Cited 10 Mar 2022

Introduction to PROV

2

2.1 Learning Objectives

The primary goal of this chapter is to introduce the PROV model and key ideas relating to PROV. In this chapter, you will learn about:

- An overview of PROV and PROV family of documents
- Different PROV serializations
- Core Components of PROV
- Examples in making a PROV document

2.2 A Provenance Story

Provenance is a description of how something has come to be. Right now you are reading this book, perhaps relaxing on your couch. Think back to how this situation came to be. Perhaps you took the bus to your local library, searched for this book in the card catalog, jotted down the call number, found the book on a particular shelf, checked it out with the librarian, and finally returned home. This would be a description of provenance; the provenance of how you came to find yourself relaxing on your couch reading this book.

Let's explore this scenario a bit more carefully and ask ourselves a few questions about what we consider to be provenance. What is the underlying structure of this description of provenance, and what are its core components? The structure is a series of steps or events, some components which led to a particular outcome, in this case, our hypothetical reader enjoying a book. This leads to other questions. Can all provenance be described as a linear sequence of steps? *Should* provenance be described as a linear sequence of steps, even if it can be? Those are questions to keep in mind as we think more deeply about provenance.

© The Author(s), under exclusive license to Springer Nature Switzerland AG 2022
R. Bettivia et al., *Documenting the Future: Navigating Provenance Metadata Standards*,
Synthesis Lectures on Information Concepts, Retrieval, and Services,
https://doi.org/10.1007/978-3-031-18700-1_2

Our provenance example also has physical things described in it, in addition to the steps. A bus, a library, a card catalog, a shelf and of course, the book. It seems that objects are also core components of provenance. Finally, there is another class of physical things in this example: people who cause the sequence of events to occur. Those would include the bus driver, the librarian and our hypothetical reader.

These three concepts: *events*, *objects* and *agents* will be the foundation for any description of provenance we attempt. The goal of this chapter, and the goal of the PROV standard, is to be more precise in what we mean by these concepts, expand upon them as necessary, and explore a vocabulary for describing how objects, events, and agents interact in narrating how something has come to be.

2.3   What is PROV?

PROV is a standard for representing provenance that was introduced by the World Wide Web Consortium (W3C) in 2013 [1]. It is more appropriate to describe PROV as a set of standards, as the PROV initiative supports and maintains a data model along with multiple serializations for XML, RDF, OWL, and other uses. This reflects on the mission of the W3C in promoting interoperability on the web: the PROV standard(s) are meant to provide human readable but machine actionable representations of provenance.

The introduction to the PROV-Overview [3] illustrates the various components of the PROV standards and their relationship to the data model (PROV-DM) [4]. In this and the following chapter, we will concentrate on the content provided in Table 2.1. This includes PROV-DM as well as the three serializations: PROV-N (PROV notation), PROV-XML, and PROV-O (Ontology, in OWL2 format). While not discussed in this book, there is also PROV-DC which is an effort to map the PROV standard onto the Dublin Core terms. The reader is

Table 2.1 Online resources available for PROV

Information	Webpage
Wikipedia	https://en.wikipedia.org/wiki/PROV_(Provenance)
Overview	http://www.w3.org/TR/2013/NOTE-prov-overview-20130430/
Data model	http://www.w3.org/TR/2013/REC-prov-dm-20130430/
Notation	http://www.w3.org/TR/2013/REC-prov-n-20130430/
Ontology	http://www.w3.org/TR/2013/REC-prov-o-20130430/
XML	http://www.w3.org/TR/2013/NOTE-prov-xml-20130430/

encouraged to make use of the valuable resources provided by the W3C; their documentation is extensive and clear. The reader is also referred to the wonderful book by Moreau and Groth [2].

2.4 Provenance with PROV

The PROV-Overview [3] describes provenance in this way:

> Provenance is information about entities, activities, and people involved in producing a piece of data or thing, which can be used to form assessments about its quality, reliability or trustworthiness.

As we see in this description, the developers of PROV focus on the three core concepts introduced at the beginning of this chapter: entities (objects), activities (events), and people (also referred to as agents).

We also notice in this description that the rationale or purpose for recording provenance is for assessing an item's "quality, reliability or trustworthiness". This aspect of provenance was discussed with respect to artwork in Chap. 1. However, quality, reliability, and trustworthiness are important in many contexts, as is provenance.

2.4.1 Making Wine, Making Provenance: The Basic PROV Model

For the remainder of this chapter, we will explore provenance and the PROV standard with the help of a *toy example*, wine making. Let us consider a hypothetical winery, *JeMiRi Winery*, which manufactures a broad selection of wines. JeMiRi Winery places great value in being open and transparent with its customers on the manufacturing processes of its family of wines. JeMiRi achieves this transparency by attaching the PROV standard to all of its activities. This public provenance serves as a testament to its wine quality.

> Definition Toy Example: A toy example is a simple model that purposefully leaves out fine details, used for teaching and explaining. We will follow some basic wine making practices in the following example, but we know there is a lot more involved in making great wine!

Recall from the PROV-Overview that provenance is a bookkeeping of entities, activities, and people involved in the production of something. If our something is wine, what would those entities, activities, and people be?

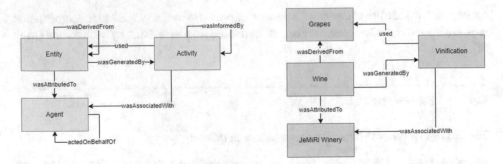

Fig. 2.1 Basic PROV model for vinification. The left-hand figure is the class diagram provided as the W3C PROV standard [4]. The right-hand figure is a data view for ascribing provenance to wine making

To begin in the simplest of terms, vinification (wine making) is the process of turning grapes into wine. This provides us with two critical entities for our provenance record: grapes and wine. Our central activity has also been defined, namely vinification. And finally, we have the JeMiRi Winery acting as the agent responsible for the vinification.

Figure 2.1 shows the general PROV data model for provenance along with our toy example.

On the left panel, PROV uses recursive relationships: each core concept has an arrow that loops back on itself. While the arrows appear to say that entities are derived from themselves or that agents are acting on behalf of themselves, the model is actually allowing for entities to be derived from other entities, activities to be informed by other activities, and agents acting on behalf of other agents when we add more core components. This is a *class diagram* for PROV. In our wine example on the right, the two entities, grapes and wine, are given distinct symbols and the relationships between the entities, activities, and agents become clearer. This is a *data diagram* using the PROV classes and relationships.

2.4.2 PROV-Notation

As mentioned in Sect. 2.3, the PROV standard supports three serializations of the DM: PROV-N, PROV-XML, and PROV-O. A simple entity such as wine would be written as follows for the three serializations.

Prov-N	Entity (wine)
PROV-XML	<prov:entity prov:id="ex:wine"/>
PROV-O	:wine a prov:entity .

Similarly, activity and agents would be written as follows.

Prov-N	activity (vinification)
PROV-XML	<prov:activity prov:id="ex:vinification"/>
PROV-O	:vinification a prov:activity .
Prov-N	agent(JeMiRi-Winery)
PROV-XML	<prov:entity prov:id="ex:JeMiri-Winery"/>
PROV-O	:jemiri-winery a prov:agent .

The XML serialization is primarily for machine representations. The OWL representation carries with it the Resource Description Framework which adds extra semantics. Note that all of the examples have PROV-XML and PROV-O serializations provided in the supplementary materials, which can be found at metaprov.org.

For the rest of this chapter we will work with PROV-N along with diagrams for understanding the PROV standard. Here, we will go over the basic structure of PROV-N. Simple components like entities, activities, and agents are succinctly described by their type with an identifier as shown in the examples above. Relationship names come from the PROV documentation and are described using a comma separated list of the entities to which the relationship holds. Note that the order in which the entities are listed within the relationship is important. For example:

```
used(vinification, grapes)
wasGeneratedBy(wine, vinification)
wasDerivedFrom(wine, grapes) // wine was derived from grapes
wasAssociatedWith(vinification, JeMiRi-Winery)
wasAttributedTo(wine, JeMiRi-Winery)
```

In these examples, our identifiers[1] are broad, human-readable names for things along the process: wine, grapes, vinification, JeMiRi-Winery. In real world provenance recording, the identifiers are likely to be numeric-based IDs such as bar codes or ISBNs.

In addition to the identifiers, each of the core components has various attributes which can be associated with it, such as the time an activity occurred or for sub-typing activities, agents, or entities. These will be introduced to our wine example as they become relevant. Let's explore our winery some more.

---

[1] There is another small but important detail about the identifiers. Notice that JeMiRi Winery is hyphenated when used in the PROV-N. This is required as part of the formal grammar which makes the notation machine readable.

2.4.3   Composite Entities or Collections

In Sect. 2.4.1 we defined vinification as the process of turning grapes into wine. Let's expand on that concept a little more. The first step to wine making is to crush the grapes. This produces a liquid (called *must*) which contains both the grape juice as well as the skins, seeds, and stems. The solid material is referred to as *pomace*.

We can add these steps to our vinification diagram as shown in Fig. 2.2. PROV does not have an explicit concept for composite entities; however, there is something very suitable called *collections*.

Collection

```
entity(must, [ prov:type='prov:Collection' ])
hadMember(must, juice)
hadMember(must, pomace)
entity(grapes)
used(pressing, grapes)
wasGeneratedBy(must, pressing)
wasDerivedFrom(must, grapes)
```

This example illustrates a few things. One is the use of the entity attribute to define must as a collection of juice and pomace. Note that in the notation, the namespace of our type definition is PROV. The *prov*:type is of a *prov*:collection. Namespacing allows for the freedom to use types or relationships from other vocabularies/ontologies within a PROV record.

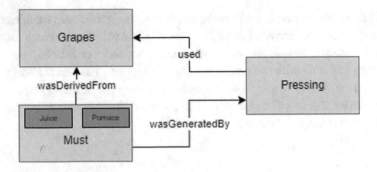

Fig. 2.2 Composite entities

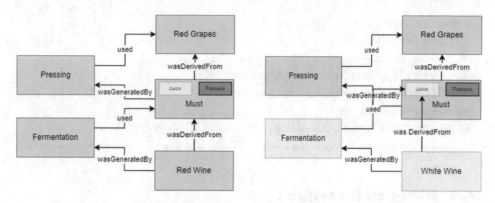

Fig. 2.3 Provenance can be linked to a collection (Must in left panel) or a member of a collection (Juice in right panel)

Definition Namespace: Namespaces provide a mechanism for scoping a term. This allows multiple vocabularies to be used together, as namespace1:type can be distinguished from namespace2:type. Namespaces are typically defined through the use of a URL to the schema or vocabulary, along with a custom abbreviation. In our example, prov would point to http://www.w3.org/ns/prov.

If no namespace is provided, the namespace of the parent document is assumed.

Another thing to note in this example is that by describing the must as a collection of juice and pomace, we can now define provenance to either the collection as a whole or using the individual pieces. Consider the example shown in Fig. 2.3 in which we can distinguish a red wine from a white wine depending on whether the pomace was used during fermentation or not.

These two scenarios could be written in PROV-N as follows:

```
entity(red-grapes)
activity(pressing)
used(pressing, red-grapes)
entity(juice)
entity(pomace)
entity(must, [ prov:type='prov:Collection' ])
hadMember(must, juice)
hadMember(must, pomace)
wasGeneratedBy(must, pressing)
activity(fermentation-red)
```

```
used(fermentation-red, must)
entity(red-wine)
wasGeneratedBy(red-wine, fermentation-red)
activity(fermentation-white)
used(fermentation-white, juice)
entity(white-wine)
wasGeneratedBy(white-wine, fermentation-white)
```

2.4.4   PROV-Notation Revisited

In the previous sections, we visualized provenance with the help of diagrams and the PROV vocabulary. We then described that view using the PROV-Notation. PROV-Notation was developed to support both human-readability in communicating provenance information as well as machine-interpretability. To accomplish these dual goals, PROV-N was designed to have a simple, technology-independent syntax which can both be parsed according to a formal grammar as well as be read by humans.

As for human-readability, the syntax is a bit awkward: it does not reflect natural human language. However, it is certainly a simple enough task to rearrange the words a bit to interpret *wasGeneratedBy(wine, vinification)* as *wine was generated by vinification*. Similarly, for (the collection) must had juice as a member.

Another goal for PROV-N was to support machine-interpretability. Trung Dong Huynh has developed and continues to maintain a Python library for PROV-N.[2] The Python library treats the core components of the PROV data model and PROV-N as Python objects of their respective classes. This allows provenance to be created, manipulated, and queried the same as any other Python code.

A translation of our latest example into Prov Python is shown below:

```
d1 = ProvDocument()
e1 = d1.entity('eg:red-grapes')
e2 = d1.entity('eg:juice')
e3 = d1.entity('eg:pomace')
e4 = d1.collection('eg:must')
e4.hadMember(e2)
e4.hadMember(e3)
e5 = d1.entity('eg:red-wine')
e6 = d1.entity('eg:white-wine')
```

---

[2] PROV-N Python Library: https://prov.readthedocs.io/en/latest/.

```
p1 = d1.activity('eg:pressing')
p2 = d1.activity('eg:fermentation-red')
p3 = d1.activity('eg:fermentation-white')
e4.wasGeneratedBy(p1)
e5.wasGeneratedBy(p2)
e6.wasGeneratedBy(p3)
p1.used(e1)
p2.used(e4)
p3.used(e2)
```

This is just an abbreviated example. A fuller example which is executable as a Python notebook can be found in the supplementary materials (metaprov.org).

Let us examine the Python snippet. The notation has been changed from the PROV-N syntax to fit with Python syntax. The developer(s) of Prov Python have mapped the PROV entities to Python objects which are accessed as standard Python objects using the Python '.' conventions.

To accommodate this, there is a top-level object called a ProvDocument in which all the prov components are embedded. For simplicity, each element of provenance is given a unique variable name using the Python prov syntax for entities, activities, collections, etc. Apart from the slight syntactical modifications, it is hoped that the Python version is similar enough to PROV-N that it is not difficult to translate between the two.

The code above simply builds a provenance record (document) within the Python virtual environment. The benefit of having done this is that it can now be manipulated using Python. For instance, a simple command:

```
print(d1.get_provn())
```

outputs the provenance record in the standard PROV-N.

```
document
prefix eg <http://www.example.org/>
entity(eg:red-grapes)
entity(eg:juice)
entity(eg:pomace)
entity(eg:must, [prov:type='prov:Collection'])
hadMember(eg:must, eg:juice)
```

```
hadMember(eg:must, eg:pomace)
entity(eg:red-wine)
entity(eg:white-wine)
activity(eg:pressing, -, -)
activity(eg:fermentation-red, -, -)
activity(eg:fermentation-white, -, -)
wasGeneratedBy(eg:must, eg:pressing, -)
wasGeneratedBy(eg:red-wine, eg:fermentation-red, -)
wasGeneratedBy(eg:white-wine, eg:fermentation-white, -)
used(eg:pressing, eg:red-grapes, -)
used(eg:fermentation-red, eg:must, -)
used(eg:fermentation-white, eg:juice, -)
endDocument
```

The above summary of our provenance record is now written in well-formed PROV-N. Note, that in the above example, we have now provided a namespace for our terms: 'eg'. The notation also provides dashes to identify those attributes which are optionally provided to the term, such as the start and end time attributes for activity.

Another benefit of this object-oriented representation for PROV-N is that we can build a graph diagram for PROV using an external package 'GraphVis'.

The following code:

```
# visualize the graph
from prov.dot import prov_to_dot
dot = prov_to_dot(d1)
dot.write_png('article-prov.png')
```

produces the graph in Fig. 2.4 shown below.

Convention: Note that in Fig. 2.4 entities are represented by yellow ovals and activities by blue rectangles. This is a recommended visualization scheme from the W3C (https://www.w3.org/2011/prov/wiki/Diagrams). There is a third shape for agents: an orange "pentagon house". This convention is used by Prov Python as shown in the figure; however, seeing that ProvONE and PREMIS do not adhere to this convention it is not used elsewhere in this book.

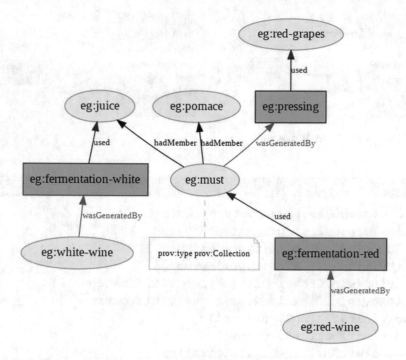

Fig. 2.4 GraphVis representation of the Prov Python document

2.5 Core Components

For the remainder of this chapter, let's return to the three core components of PROV, activities, entities, and agents, and explore them in more detail. Particularly, we will focus on the role each of these components play in an object's provenance by considering variations in the entities, agents, or activities.

2.5.1 Entity View

Entity-centric provenance was already discussed in the context of composite entities (PROV collections). The general idea is that a difference in entities along a provenance chain may have different outcomes even if the activities and agents are unchanged. In the composite entity example, whether our fermentation process used the must or the juice changed the type of wine produced. Thus, that portion of the graph was critical for our provenance.

Another similar example is shown in Fig. 2.5 where we change the type of grapes used for vinification. When the type of grape changes, so does the type of wine. This can be written succinctly using PROV-N as below:

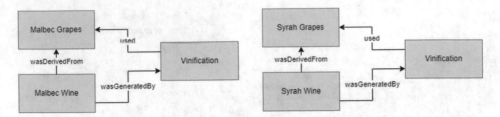

Fig. 2.5 Provenance dependent on entity type

```
entity(grapes1, [ grape:type='Malbec' ])
entity(grapes2, [ grape:type='Syrah' ])
entity(wine1, [ wine:type='Malbec' ])
entity(wine2, [ wine:type='Syrah' ])
activity(vinification1, [ type='Vinification' ])
activity(vinification2, [ type='Vinification' ])
used(vinification1, grapes1)
used(vinification2, grapes2)
wasGeneratedBy(wine1, vinification1)
wasGeneratedBy(wine2, vinification2)
wasDerivedFrom(wine1, grapes1)
wasDerivedFrom(wine2, grapes2)
```

Notice that in this example, we need different identifiers for each of the entities and activities regarding grapes, wine, and wine-making. This is because we are now distinguishing between particular instances of things and not simply classes of things: not grapes in general, but *grape 1* for *Malbec* and *grape 2* for *Syrah*. This was true in the red wine/white wine example, but we were able to get away with the class names as *must* is a collection while *juice* is a member in the collection. This will be discussed more in the next chapter on Advanced PROV, including how we can use attributes like "type" shown above to group specific provenance instances into provenance classes.

2.5.2 Activity View

The previous section provides an example of how changing the entity in two otherwise identical processes changes the outcome. The same holds for changes in process. In the following example, the type of grapes remain the same, and we do not distinguish between must, juice, or pomace. Rather, the distinction between sparkling wine and a traditional chardonnay arises from a second fermentation process (Fig. 2.6).

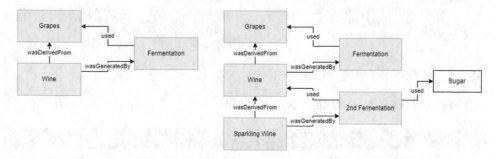

Fig. 2.6 Provenance dependent on process type

```
entity(grapes)
entity(wine)
entity(sparkling-wine)
entity(sugar)
activity(fermentation1, [ type='Fermentation' ])
activity(fermentation2, [ type='Fermentation' ])
used(fermentation1, grapes)
used(fermentation2, wine)
used(fermentation2, sugar)
wasGeneratedBy(wine, fermentation1)
wasGeneratedBy(sparkling-wine, fermentation2)
wasDerivedFrom(wine, grapes)
wasDerivedFrom(sparkling-wine, wine)
```

Another classic wine example where changing an aspect of the process is the difference between Champagne and other sparkling wines which use the méthode champenoise but are not produced in the Champagne region of France. This is illustrated in Fig. 2.7 and introduces the optional attribute "loc" applied to the activity.

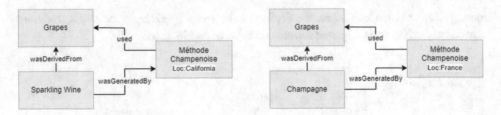

Fig. 2.7 Provenance dependent on location

The PROV-N for this is example is shown below:

```
entity(grapes)
entity(champagne)
entity(sparkling-wine)
activity(méthode-champenoise1, [
  prov:location="Napa, California" ])
activity(méthode-champenoise2, [
  prov:location="Champagne, France" ])
used(méthode-champenoise1, grapes)
used(méthode-champenoise2, grapes)
wasGeneratedBy(sparkling-wine, méthode-champenoise1)
wasGeneratedBy(champagne, méthode-champenoise2)
```

2.5.3   Agent View

To return to the last of our three core components, agents, the provenance of the final product also depends on the agents along the chain. This is a key component in distinguishing genuine products from counterfeits. Was that watch truly manufactured by Rolex or is it a timepiece which was built from the same parts and using the same process but by a different company?

The importance of agency when considering the provenance of products or merchandise is worth considering further. If the preceding question was actually being asked, would it truly matter if the agent was different as long as the parts (entities) and process (activities) were identical? This is a complicated question as product branding has its own perceived value irrespective of the final product. However, in addition to simple brand recognition, the brand can be used as a judgement of quality in itself. That is to say, a customer may inherently trust the process of manufacturer A over manufactured B. In a sense, the value judgement placed on the brand functions as a proxy for an examination of the provenance to genuinely attest to the quality. Provenance is a narrative whose storyline arises as much from the provenance recorder as from properties inherent to the object.

Lastly, there is another important reason for the recording of agents in provenance. Assuming the provenance record may be used for quality control, identifying key agents along the chain, whether they be people, software, robots, or organizations, can be used in identifying and controlling for mistakes throughout the production process.

2.6 Mini-Exercise

This section is a chance for you to apply your knowledge and understanding of provenance and the PROV standard. Below are a list of products similar to the wine-making example used throughout this chapter. For this exercise, you should build a PROV provenance record for the various example products paying particular attention to the specification. That is, in the case of Belgian Chocolate for instance, what provenance details would be needed to distinguish it from other types of chocolate?

This table is provided to help guide you in your task by first identifying the core components of the provenance record you are building: entities, activities, and agents.

Product	Entities	Activities	Agents
Grass-fed Beef			
Free-range chicken			
Kosher salt			
Decaffeinated coffee			
Belgian chocolate			

Discussion: Some of these examples are more difficult than others. The point of the exercise is to explore provenance concepts on your own. There are many "correct" answers and some of the difficulties with these examples will be tackled in the following chapter on Advanced PROV.

Hopefully you have focused on entities, activities, and agents which help characterize the qualified aspect of the product. For instance, Belgian chocolate appears to be distinguished by the location of the activity (as the champagne example), but of course could indicate a "Belgian Method". Similarly, Kosher tends to designate an association with a religious authority, although not necessarily for Kosher salt! Finally, decaffeinating, free-ranging, and grass-feeding all imply activities but where in the provenance record do they appear?

2.7 Summary

This chapter covered the three core concepts of provenance-entities, activities and agents-in the context of the PROV standard(s) maintained by the W3C. Those three core components are foundational to provenance and provenance metadata and can also be found in the PREMIS standard (as objects, events and agents).

References

1. Moreau L, Groth P, Cheney J, Lebo T, Miles S (2015) The rationale of PROV. J Web Semant 35:235–257
2. Moreau L, Groth P (2013) Provenance: an introduction to PROV. Synth Lect Semant Web: Theory Technol 3:1–129
3. https://www.w3.org/TR/prov-overview/
4. https://www.w3.org/TR/2013/REC-prov-dm-20130430/

PROV Advanced Topics

3

3.1 Learning Objectives

The primary goal of this chapter is to introduce more advanced topics in the PROV model. In this chapter, you will learn about:

- PROV relationships for generation, usage, and derivation
- PROV alternates and specializations
- PROV bundles and plans

3.2 Introduction

In the last chapter, provenance was defined as the way something has come to be. This history or lineage of an object of interest was decomposed into the three core components of the PROV data model: entities, activities, and agents. A wine-making example explored these concepts and their relationships in more detail while illustrating how various serializations of the PROV-DM [1], such as PROV-N, can be used to record the provenance of something. The chapter concluded with some exercises on which aspects of provenance and those core components are useful for verifying or assuring the quality of some common household products.

This chapter will cover three more advanced topics of provenance, once again exploring their use within the W3C PROV family of standards [2]. The first will be the important semantic considerations required for defining *entities*, *activities*, and *agents*. One aspect of this, the distinction between classes and instances, was touched upon in Sect. 2.5.1 with regards to the example of distinguishing Malbec wine from Syrah. Keeping track of levels of abstraction as is the case for classes versus instances is one semantic concern; however, there

R. Bettivia et al., *Documenting the Future: Navigating Provenance Metadata Standards*, Synthesis Lectures on Information Concepts, Retrieval, and Services, https://doi.org/10.1007/978-3-031-18700-1_3

will be many others. For instance, various entities which are related to activities can take on
different roles in the activity. It requires care in building the provenance graph to preserve
these distinctions. There are many other roles and semantic distinctions for which PROV
also has terms that will be explored in this chapter. Once again, the reader is encouraged to
explore the wonderful documentation provided by the W3C [2] as well as those by Moreau
et al. [3, 4].

The second topic is that of *prospective provenance*. The previous chapter defined provenance as the way something has come to be. That definition and the concepts associated with
it are sufficient if we are concerned about the provenance of one specific object. For instance,
in the case of works of art, we are interested in the chain of custody of a particular painting
in order to assure its authenticity. This particular type of provenance is called *retrospective
provenance*.

However, provenance is more expansive than just retrospective analysis. Perhaps we
not only want to know how a particular object has come to be, but we also want a recipe
for making more. This concept is referred to as prospective provenance. We introduce the
distinction between retrospective and prospective provenance here and discuss them further
in Chap. 4 and in Chap. 7.

The third topic will be considering the consequences of the *Open World Assumption*
(OWA) versus the *Closed World Assumption* (CWA).[1] With the CWA, it is assumed that
everything that is "true" about a system is defined within it. For instance, when querying the
employee table of a database, it is assumed that a record for every current employee exists
within the database. This allows us to draw conclusions about the absence of items. With
the OWA, it is assumed that the information in the system is true; however, there can be
many other true facts which are not recorded within the system. When crafting a provenance
record, care must be taken to explicitly define what is known to be true as well as what is
known to be false, if that information is important for provenance.

This chapter will begin by revisiting the relationships between the three core PROV
components and then move on to additional PROV terms and concepts. The three broad
topics of semantics, prospective versus retrospective provenance, and OWA versus CWA
will be highlighted throughout this discussion.

3.3   PROV Relationships

In the preceding chapter we illustrated how the core components are related to each other to
produce a provenance chain. Specifically, we used the relationships *used* and *wasGenerat-
edBy* to connect entities with activities; *wasDerivedFrom* to connect entities with each other;
and *wasAttributedTo* and *wasAssociatedWith* to associate agents with entities and activities,
respectively.

---

[1] https://en.wikipedia.org/wiki/Closed-world_assumption.

Each of these terms for relationships has a specific definition provided in the PROV standard. The previous chapter did not specify these formal definitions, as common usage of the words was sufficient. Such human-readability for provenance was one of the design goals of PROV. It is time to consider the definitions from the PROV standard [1], starting with the entities, activities, and agents.

- An **entity** is a physical, digital, conceptual, or other kind of thing with some fixed aspects; entities may be real or imaginary.
- An **activity** is something that occurs over a period of time and acts upon or with entities.
- An **agent** is something that bears some form of responsibility for an activity taking place, for the existence of an entity, or for another agent's activity. An agent may be a particular type of entity or activity. This means that the model can be used to express provenance of the agents themselves.

These definitions allow for the uses described in the preceding chapter, along with the various observations of classes versus instances and concrete objects versus conceptual objects. Agents have not been discussed much up to now; however, the suggested usage has been for people or other groups such as organizations. The PROV standard allows for agents to be responsible for both entities and activities, but a subtle addition also allows for them to *be* either entities or activities [3]. An agent can be an activity, so in principle a process such as a *democratic vote* [2] could be responsible for another activity such as the election of an official.

The previous paragraph defined the PROV classes; the following will define the PROV relationships between these classes. Below are the PROV definitions [1] for *generation*, *usage* and *derivation*.

- **Generation** is the completion of production of a new entity by an activity. This entity did not exist before generation and becomes available for usage after this generation.
- **Usage** is the beginning of utilizing an entity by an activity. Before usage, the activity had not begun to utilize this entity and could not have been affected by the entity.
- A **derivation** is a transformation of an entity into another, an update of an entity resulting in a new one, or the construction of a new entity based on a pre-existing entity.

---

[2] As a thought exercise, if one wanted to associate each of the individual voters to the process of the democratic vote, would all of the voters be associated with the final outcome or only the portion which voted for the winner?

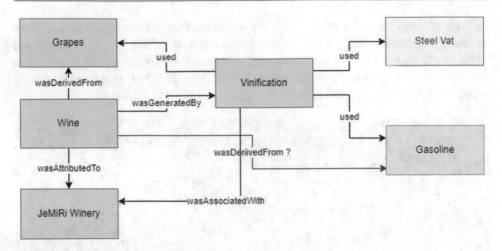

Fig. 3.1 Illustration of different semantic roles for *usage*

The definitions of generation and usage should be intuitive and agree with the examples in the preceding chapter. Activities can use entities and they can generate entities. The term derivation, however, requires some consideration. In the wine making example, vinification used grapes to generate wine and therefore wine is considered to be *derived* from grapes. In this context, it would be appropriate to say that the grapes were transformed into wine, or that the wine was based on the pre-existing grapes.

Usage is a more general term than the terms *transformation*, *updating* or *basing*. As an example, consider a more verbose provenance record for wine making in which case we wish to specify that the wine was fermented in a steel vat, and that required refrigeration which used gasoline as a fuel for the compressor. In this more detailed example, we could create the provenance graph shown in Fig. 3.1.

In this case, the activity of vinification is shown to have used grapes (as an ingredient for the wine), a steel vat (as equipment), and gasoline (as a fuel source for the activity).

This graph presents an obvious question / dilemma. In the basic PROV examples, the input (used) entities and output (generated) entities of a single activity stood in a derivation relationship. What about in this case? Is it fair to claim that the wine was derived from a steel vat? Certainly the choice of a steel vat over an oak barrel will affect the wine—but is that effect a derivation relationship? Similarly, is it fair to claim that the wine was derived from gasoline?

Take Home: Derivation cannot be inferred from a usage and generation alone. It must be explicitly stated in the provenance record. Similarly, due to the OWA, failure to specify that a derivation relationship exists does not imply that one entity was not derived from the other. Care must be taken if this type of provenance information is deemed important.

This example can be defined using the following PROV-Notation which results in the provenance graph shown in Fig. 3.2.

```
entity(wine)
entity(grapes)
entity(gasoline)
entity(steel-vat)
agent(JeMiRi-Winery)
activity(Vinification)
wasAttributedTo(wine, JeMiRi-Winery)
wasDerivedFrom(wine, grapes)
wasGeneratedBy(wine, Vinification)
used(Vinification, grapes, [ prov:role="ingredient" ])
used(Vinification, gasoline, [
prov:role="temp-regulation" ])
used(Vinification, steel-vat, [ prov:role="container" ])
```

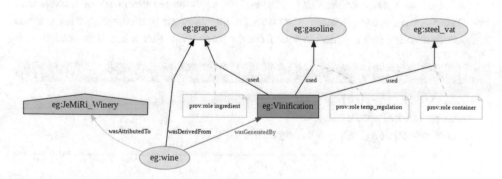

Fig. 3.2 Python PROV figure of example of usage

3.4   Alternate and Specialization

While the wine-making examples of PROV are designed to walk the reader through uses of
PROV, the individual examples have jumped through different levels of abstraction. In some
cases vinification refers to a general process (Fig 2.1) while in others it refers to a specific
process applied to a specific set of ingredients (Fig 2.4). In other real world cases, it is likely
that this will be fine-tuned further such that individual lots or batches of wine would be
tracked with suitable IDs and timestamps, and each individual run of the fermenter would
also be tracked at a time-stamped instance level.

There is another overlapping issue regarding levels of abstraction: how to allow two
different provenance recorders to refer to the same "thing" in a provenance record but at
different levels of abstraction. For instance, perhaps at the organizational level, the management is only concerned with the different wine products of JeMiRi Winery while at the
quality control department, they are concerned about the individual lots and batches. PROV
[4] provides two mechanisms to support this: *alternates* and *specializations*.

- Two **alternate** entities present aspects of the same thing. These aspects may be the
  same or different, and the alternate entities may or may not overlap in time.
- An entity that is a **specialization** of another shares all aspects of the latter, and additionally presents more specific aspects of the same thing as the latter. In particular,
  the lifetime of the entity being specialized contains that of any specialization.

As is true with much of the PROV standard, these items are designed for flexible use.
For example, we can use alternate in the wine making example to distinguish wine that has
finished fermenting and is stored in a vat from the same wine after it has been bottled.

```
entity(syrah-vat)
entity(syrah-bottle)
alternateOf(syrah-vat, syrah-bottle)
```

The implication here is that the two entities refer to the same thing, in this case the
Syrah wine. The storage vessel is different and this distinction can be captured, when it is
important, via the two distinct entities. The alternate relationship maintains that they are
two different representations of the same thing. One can go a step further and create a single
entity for Syrah which is an alternate of both.

```
entity(syrah)
entity(syrah-vat)
entity(syrah-bottle)
alternateOf(syrah, syrah-vat)
alternateOf(syrah, syrah-bottle)
```

The latter example might benefit from the use of the specialization relationship. Remember that in the specialization relationship, the specialized member has all of the same properties of the general entity, plus additional attributes which serve to sub-class it. In the case of the Syrah example, the specialized entities of syrah-vat and syrah-bottle would share all the same properties of the general Syrah wine, but they would have additional attributes for their storage location. The two specialized entities would be considered alternates of one another. Indeed, one could imagine that the wine is bottled from a vat and subsequently poured back into the vat without change to the wine itself.[3]

```
entity(syrah)
entity(syrah-vat)
entity(syrah-bottle)
specializationOf(syrah-vat, syrah)
specializationOf(syrah-bottle, syrah)
alternateOf(syrah-vat, syrah-bottle)
```

Question: We noted in the previous section that derivation cannot be inferred from a transitive application of usage and generation. What about alternatives, are they symmetric? If A is an alternate of B, is B guaranteed to also be an alternate of A, or must both relationships be made explicit?
Discussion: Alternate is a symmetric relationship; however, specialization is not.

3.5 Provenance Levels

Provenance is a description of how something came to be. Chapter 2 began with a hypothetical example of how you came to be reading this book. In that provenance description,

---

[3] At least with respect to this being a *toy* example!

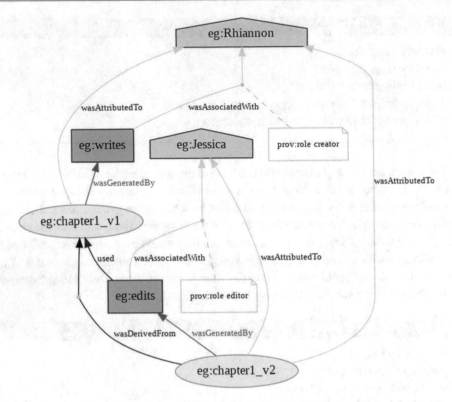

Fig. 3.3 Hypothetical provenance of Chap. 1 of *Documenting the Future*. The original draft was written by Rhiannon (*creator*) and subsequently edited by Jessica (*editor*). The edited chapter (*chapter1_v2*) is attributed to both authors

the book was only a single entity in the larger provenance tale which contained a library, a bus, and other sundries. One could ask not only how you came to be reading the book, but also, how did the book come to be in the first place? This would require digging deeper into the provenance of a single entity within the larger provenance record. If such "book" provenance exists, it might look something like Fig. 3.3.

This provenance description is similar to the W3C examples of PROV. In this fictitious example, provenance is used to record the history of how the book was compiled, which authors wrote which chapters, who created the figures, who edited the manuscript, and who compiled the final manuscript for submission to the publisher.

There is a different perspective between the provenance of how the book was created versus how a reader came to be reading the book. The domains of interest are different. A reader may not be interested in the different software tools required for writing text versus illustrating figures, or how to manage version control of various edits. The reader may only be interested in the book's availability (whether the local library has a copy), its accessibility (whether there is a hardcover version), and the book's content (ratings from other readers).

An important aspect of provenance is that irrespective of the differing perspectives of various provenance narratives, they can be stitched together. The important question for those creating a provenance record is which perspectives should be included, which should be omitted, and most importantly, which perspectives should be connected. Provenance needs its own appraisal process; we will revisit this idea again in Chap. 6 in the context of environments in PREMIS.

Note that this is not simply a consideration for provenance, but for any modeling technique which allows multiple levels of abstraction. As an example, if one creates a relational database table for Books, every Book record in the table is of the same kind. They are each forced to share the same schema, the same attributes, and each book exists on the same semantic level even if the contents are vastly different.

Title	Authors	Publisher	Publication date
Harry Potter and the Chamber of Secrets	J. K. Rowling	Bloomsbury	1998
Documenting the Future	R. Bettivia, Y. Cheng, M.Gryk	Springer	2022
A Brief History of Time	S. Hawking	Bantam	1988
Locke and Key	J. Hill	IDW Publishing	2008

Contrast this with an RDF description of the world. For RDF, there is complete freedom to connect objects via arbitrary relationships of various levels of abstraction. For instance, one could easily construct the following RDF[4]:

```
:Charlie_Brown :owns :Snoopy.
:Snoopy :befriends :Woodstock .
:Woodstock :hasColor :Yellow .
:Snoopy a :dog .
:Snoopy a :fictional_character .
:Charles_Schultz :created :Snoopy .
```

This set of RDF triples connects various aspects of the Peanuts work from different real-world and fictional perspectives, in some cases spanning both. Snoopy is a dog only in the fictional world; Charles Schultz created Snoopy only in the real world; yet Woodstock is yellow in both the fictional and real worlds.

---

[4] This is described using Turtle format (https://www.w3.org/TR/turtle/).

For the remainder of this chapter, we will explore various perspectives of provenance. To start, we will explore the provenance of provenance.

3.6   Provenance of Provenance

One perspective on provenance which is often important is the provenance of the provenance record itself. If provenance is a proxy for trustworthiness or quality, then the provenance of provenance is a proxy for the trustworthiness of the provenance record, or a proxy for the proxy. There are two perspectives on the provenance of provenance which are supported explicitly by PROV, the concepts of *bundles* and *plans*.

3.6.1   Bundles

Bundles are similar in a sense to collections in that they are entities which represent a combination of provenance items. The definition of collection [4] is provided below.

- A **collection** is an entity that provides a structure to some constituents that must themselves be entities. These constituents are said to be **members** of the collections. An **empty collection** is a collection without members.
- **Membership** is the belonging of an entity to a collection.

There are three critical differences between collections and bundles. One, a collection can only contain entities while a bundle can contain an entire provenance record. Two, collections have the *hasMember* relationship (as they contain only entities) while bundles have no such pointer to the individual bundle contents. Three, and most importantly, bundles implicitly and explicitly contain provenance. In that respect, they are a specialized type of entity: while PROV entities can be anything—grapes, bottles, works of art—bundles are always a record of provenance. Therefore, any provenance related to bundles is the provenance of provenance. Here is the definition [4] of a bundle.

A **bundle** is a named set of provenance descriptions, and is itself an entity, so allowing provenance of provenance to be expressed.

Recall how in Chap. 2, the concept of must was created as a collection of juice and pomace. This collection entity was useful as it allowed provenance relationships to connect either to the individual components (members), juice or pomace, as well as to the must as a whole.

Bundles on the other hand, exist at a different level of abstraction. Bundles are ways of referring to portions of the provenance record, not as components, but as provenance itself. For instance, the winemaker may be in charge of the fermentation process, while an accountant or auditor is responsible for documenting individual fermentation runs. Recording provenance at multiple levels of abstraction is always allowed within PROV; bundles provide an explicit mechanism where the provenance of provenance is concerned.

3.6.2 Plans

Bundles are used for documenting the provenance of provenance, that is to say, documenting how the provenance document came to be. There is another aspect of the provenance of provenance: documenting the protocol or recipe that a person or agent intended to follow during a process. The PROV entity for referring to such a recipe is a plan [4].

- A **plan** is an entity that represents a set of actions or steps intended by one or more agents to achieve some goals.
- An activity **association** is an assignment of responsibility to an agent for an activity, indicating that the agent had a role in the activity. It further allows for a plan to be specified, which is the plan intended by the agent to achieve some goals in the context of this activity.

Note in the second bullet point that the plan entity is recorded as part of the activity association relationship. It is insufficient to say there was a recipe for making Syrah wine; it must be documented that the activity of vinification was associated to an agent (the vintner) as well as the plan (or recipe). That is not to say that plans can only be associated with people. Computer code could be considered a plan and associated with a software agent or even a robotic assembly line.

An important thing to note about plans is that they are the recipe for creating something; they are not the historical lineage of how something was created. Consider a hypothetical example of a chemistry student preparing a buffer (a solution able to neutralize small amounts of an acid or base). The protocol states that one mole of sodium chloride should be added to one liter of water. The student prepares the buffer and notes in their log book that 58.6 g of NaCl was added to 990 mL of water. In this case, the plan was for creating a 1 M solution but the recorded provenance demonstrates the solution is actually 1.01 M.[5] The plan is a mechanism of recording the intent along with the outcome.

---

[5] This may or may not make a difference for the uses of the solution.

3.7   Prospective Versus Retrospective

The distinction between plans and historical provenance in the preceding section is a distinction between prospective and retrospective provenance. Prospective provenance refers
to a protocol for how to make something come to be. Retrospective provenance refers to the
lineage of how something has come to be. There is an obvious connection between the two
concepts, namely, that both types of provenance use the same underlying core components:
entities, activities, and agents. The difference is one of perspective. Is the process something which happened at a previous date and time (retrospective) or is it a prescription for
something which can be done in the future (prospective)?

At one level, prospective provenance can be considered a generalization of retrospective
provenance. Recall the definition of specialization in PROV—the specialized version has
the same attributes as the general version but also contains extra attributes. Those extra
attributes in the context of retrospective provenance would be the date or time stamp included
for a historic activity as well as items such as the actual recorded mass in the chemistry
example. We will further explore this notion embodied in a workflow management system in
Chap. 7. It is also the motivation and rationale for the ProvONE extension to PROV, which
is the topic of the next chapter.

3.8   Mini-Exercise

This section is a chance for you to test your knowledge and understanding of provenance
and the PROV standard. Section 7.2 covered alternatives and specialization using the wine
example. Use the PROV concepts of *entities*, *alternateOf* and *specializationOf* to relate the
following concepts to each other:

- aardvark
- bat
- human
- mammal
- monkey
- person
- primate

Make as full use of *specializationOf* and *alternateOf* as you can. At the end of this
exercise consider the following question. Derivation cannot be inferred solely from usage
and generation. If there are two specializations of the same general entity, are the two
specializations automatically alternates of each other?

Discussion: In this exercise you have been asked to build a taxonomy. Taxonomies are
hierarchical classification schemes in which items (or classes) are grouped based on having

similar characteristics. Specialization is a relationship for descending the hierarchy as you should have been able to do for mammals to primates to humans. In this example, two species are referred to by a synonym (alternateOf) but the other species are not alternate names for each other.

3.9 Summary

This chapter covered several advanced concepts of provenance in the context of the PROV standard(s) maintained by the W3C. The first were provenance relationships such as usage, generation, derivation, attribution, specializations, and alternatives. Finally, the provenance of provenance section covered retrospective provenance (in the context of bundles) and prospective provenance (in the context of plans). Retrospective and prospective provenance play very important roles in provenance capture and feature prominently in the following chapter on ProvONE and the use case in Chap. 7.

References

1. https://www.w3.org/TR/2013/REC-prov-dm-20130430/
2. https://www.w3.org/TR/prov-overview/
3. Moreau L, Groth P, Cheney J, Lebo T, Miles S (2015) The rationale of PROV. J Web Semant 35:235–257
4. Moreau L, Groth P (2013) Provenance: an introduction to PROV. Synth Lect Semant Web: Theory Technol 3:1–129

ProvONE

4

4.1 Learning Objectives

The primary goal of this chapter is to introduce the ProvONE model and the practical use
of it. In this chapter, you will learn about:

- A brief description of provenance related models
- The main classes of ProvONE
- How to implement ProvONE main classes in simple cases

4.2 Introduction

When you hear the word *provenance*, what are some of the first things you think of? Sotheby's
and a long lost da Vinci? A Rothko or a Pollock at the Knoedler Gallery?[1] Rudy Kurniawan
and his rare wines?[2] Neil Caffrey and the White Collar crimes?[3]

Our basic definition for provenance is a description of how something came to be. The
concept of provenance is a prevalent part of determining the authenticity of an item, whether
we are discerning the chains of custody of art or wines; or more conceptually, the genealogy
of families, the ages of rocks, or the tree of life. Provenance is often associated with the
origins or history of things.

With the current ubiquity of technology and the exponential growth of data, the provenance of an item is no longer tied to its physical properties only, but also to its digital

---

[1] https://en.wikipedia.org/wiki/Knoedler.

[2] https://en.wikipedia.org/wiki/Rudy_Kurniawan.

[3] https://en.wikipedia.org/wiki/White_Collar_(TV_series).

© The Author(s), under exclusive license to Springer Nature Switzerland AG 2022   41
R. Bettivia et al., *Documenting the Future: Navigating Provenance Metadata Standards*,
Synthesis Lectures on Information Concepts, Retrieval, and Services,
https://doi.org/10.1007/978-3-031-18700-1_4

properties. Creating standardized documentation and records for digital items is increasingly important. Many provenance and preservation metadata standards are designed for the purpose of supporting the description of physical items, digital items, and the interplay between them. Provenance can be used to demonstrate the pipeline of how a digital item, data, output, or even a conceptual idea, arises. In other words, provenance may not just be used to describe what *did* happen (retrospective provenance), it can also be used to describe what *will* happen (prospective provenance).

The scientific community increasingly aims to make science and research more transparent and reproducible, especially in fields that are reliant on computational models or scripting languages. To capture both retrospective and prospective provenance in scientific research, we document the answers to questions like: What input data went into the study? What were the parameters? What were the dependencies and versions of libraries used? What were the exact steps in our computation? Can other people reproduce the research results?

For instance, a molecular biologist working on DNA replication research might want to have means to take note of the genetic markings of a particular DNA strand and the exact calibrations of the lab equipment they have been using to compute the DNA replica outcomes. A chemist documenting the steps of crystallization of a certain chemical might use a computer program to simulate previously published results to ensure they use the right compounds and parameters.

Though many examples relating to computation and computational reproducibility come from the sciences, it is important to note that the reproducibility crisis [1] transcends disciplines. To determine the correct authorship of Shakespeare's work, researchers in digital humanities have been utilizing text mining methods to analyze word usage and other linguistic patterns [2, 3]. It is also equally crucial to document preprocessing steps, the variables, and the classifier the researchers used, in order to re-implement the same pipeline in other, similar digital humanities research (e.g. to determine authorship of another unknown work).

The idea of provenance as both history and workflow is what the ProvONE conceptual model is about. In the previous chapter, we learned that PROV is a vocabulary used to document the history of an item. The ProvONE model builds on the W3C PROV standard and provides vocabularies for bridging prospective and retrospective provenance. In this chapter, we will first discuss related models that led to the birth of ProvONE. Then, we will dive deeper into the differences between *prospective* and *retrospective* provenance. Finally, we will introduce the main classes used in ProvONE.

4.3 ProvONE Related Models

Before ProvONE, there were others models and standards to address the steps used in scientific workflows. The P-Plan Ontology, released in March 2014 and written in OWL2, is a PROV and PROV-O extension for representing scientific processes. P-Plan connects *p-plan:Step*, *p-plan:Variable*, and *p-plan:Plan* to existing PROV core classes (prov:Entity, prov:Activity), and calls the PROV classes a P-Plan (or PROV) Bundle. In this model, P-Plan concepts are the processing steps and plans that are used in a scientific workflow, whereas the PROV concepts are the execution of these steps. The full P-Plan Ontology can be found in [4].

The Open Provenance Model for Workflows (OPMW), released in December 2014, extends its predecessors OPM, PROV, and P-Plan to further introduce the concept of *workflow template* in OWL ontology. Workflow template is the design of a workflow, or the processing steps of an execution. The *workflow template* enables OPMW to model how concepts in the executable workflow correspond to the *abstract workflow* and to provide metadata for the agent(s), the creator(s) or contributor(s), related to a specific program. The full OPMW Ontology can be found in [5].

DataONE-OPM (D-OPM) is the closest precursor to ProvONE since both models were created by the DataONE community. First published in 2012, D-OPM aims to depict the basics of existing scientific workflow systems such as Kepler, Taverna, and VisTrail. D-OPM takes a relational database perspective and uses standard UML. D-OPM introduced special concepts such as *workflow structure*, *workflow traces*, *data structure*, and *workflow evolution* which inform the concepts in ProvONE. The D-OPM model can be found in [6].

ProvONE, developed by the DataONE community, is an extension to the W3C PROV standard, developed by the DataONE community. ProvONE is a conceptual model that captures different aspects of scientific workflows and is implemented in RDF (Fig. 4.1) [7]. ProvONE marks an advancement over previous models because it encodes aspects of provenance for data products that the other models have not captured. The three major provenance aspects in ProvONE are: *prospective provenance*, *retrospective provenance*, and *data structure*. We will highlight each of these aspects in the following sections.

4.4   Prospective and Retrospective Provenance

As an extension of the W3C PROV standard, ProvONE provides vocabulary for *hybrid provenance* and the data structure of the workflows. This means that ProvONE aims to bridge both prospective and retrospective provenance, hence "hybrid", while providing insights into what the data inputs and outputs are. But what exactly do we mean by retrospective and prospective in this context? We introduced these concepts in Chap. 3, and here we will explore them in more detail.

Retrospective provenance is how we usually think of provenance: lineages of items, history of events, or origins of things. It focuses on describing past activities, or the execution of events. In other words, retrospective provenance attends to the classes of the steps executed and addresses what was actually done in a process. For instance, in a data cleaning task for a dataset, the steps performed to clean columns and rows in a tabular dataset, and the runtime log files of the data cleaning software are considered retrospective provenance.

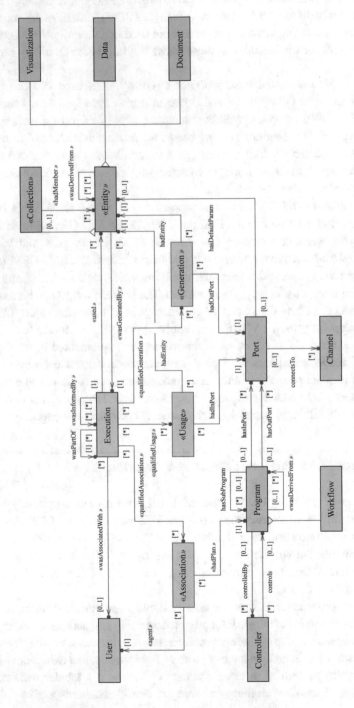

Fig. 4.1 ProvONE model with prospective provenance, retrospective provenance, process provenance, and data structure aspect

While retrospective provenance might look like a reiteration of two synonymous words, it makes clear that provenance requires a qualifier to speak to the specific temporal space of the events being recorded. Labeling provenance as retrospective speaks to past events and opens a space to speak about prospective provenance, future or possible events.

Prospective provenance conceives of provenance as a plan, a workflow, or a recipe. It describes future execution activities, or what will be done in a process. For instance, in the same data cleaning tasks mentioned earlier, the steps one plans to perform on the dataset are prospective provenance. One might ask then: how would we know what should happen in the future if we have not done it yet? Prospective provenance expands traditional conceptions of provenance and makes explicit that provenance is not a one-way street. Rather, prospective provenance enables us to better describe the ways in which the description of how a thing came to be can be both iterative and continuous. The same data cleaning steps performed and deemed as retrospective can then become the recipe for prospective cleaning plans for future datasets (Fig. 4.2). At other times, when processes are not as iterative, researchers could utilize the concept of prospective provenance to showcase their proposed plans and craft the pipeline of what will be done.

Prospective provenance in PROV is limited to the plan concept, introduced in Chap. 3. While this advanced concept enables the description of potential workflows, PROV plans are discrete entities, providing no specialized vocabulary for describing the classes of a plan such as what materials are in the plan or what set of activities comprise the plan.

The PROV family of standards aims to support eScience communities. eScience represents a huge array of disciplines with different research products, procedural norms, and publication practices. For some research domains, provenance is not merely metadata about what happened in an experiment or computation: providing a record of retrospective provenance is the actual research outcome, it is the data rather than the metadata. Chapter 2 introduced the PROV standard. In PROV, the activities and entities both represent retrospective provenance. Within a scientific workflow, activities describe processes and computations, while the latter describes the data consumed or produced during the run of a workflow.

In other eScience domains, a more holistic view of workflows is necessary to document and communicate research methods and processes. When showing what should happen, when sharing a plan for others to reproduce your work, PROV alone is not enough to describe workflows or prospective provenance.

ProvONE enables more explicit descriptions of hybrid provenance. In a computational workflow setting, having hybrid provenance means that we do not just annotate and document the past, we also construct the plans that could ideally enhance reproducibility of a research project in the future.

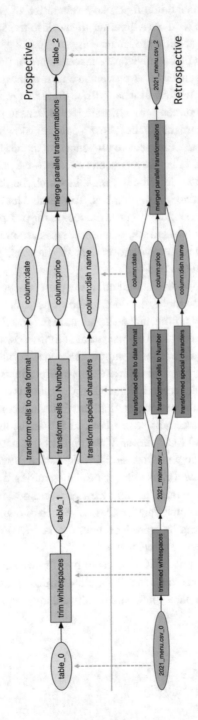

Fig. 4.2 An example of hybrid provenance from a data cleaning task

4.5   Main Classes

A complete list of ProvONE classes is in the ProvONE official document [7]. Here we highlight the three different aspects in ProvONE: *data structure*, *trace*, *workflow*. We will bring forward some of the important classes with illustrative examples.

4.5.1   Data Structure

As shown in the previous section, provenance moves in more than one temporal direction. Many provenance models and standards have included aspects of retrospective and prospective provenance. ProvONE uses the Data Structure to talk about both how data is used (inputs) and how it is produced (outputs) within a scientific workflow. The data structure includes three kinds of artifacts: the Data class, the Visualization class, and the Document class (see Fig. 4.3). *Data*, *Visualization*, and *Document* are all subclasses of prov:Entity. We can see this represented in both the graph model in Fig. 4.3 and in the code block below.

ProvONE Data Structure classes in RDF

```
provone:Data rdfs:subClassOf prov:Entity
provone:Visualization rdfs:subClassOf prov:Entity
provone:Document rdfs:subClassOf prov:Entity
```

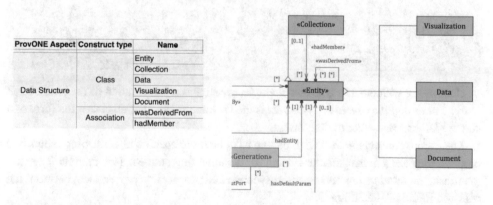

Fig. 4.3 Data Structure aspect in ProvONE. Left: ProvONE elements table. Right: Corresponding section in ProvONE model

In ProvONE, the Data class is defined as [7]:

> A **Data** item represents the basic unit of information consumed or produced by a Program. Multiple Data items may be grouped into a Collection.

For example, if we are performing topic modeling on the book *Harry Potter and the Chamber of Secrets*, the Data is the text of the book. Depending on the unit of analysis, the Data can be words, phrases, sentences, or paragraphs.

The Visualization class is defined as [7]:

> A **Visualization** item represents a basic unit of information consumed or produced by a Program, in the form of a digital visual represention. Multiple Visualization items may be grouped into a Collection.

For example, if we are performing an Optical Character Recognition (OCR) scanning of the book *Harry Potter and the Chamber of Secrets*, a Visualization could be a scanned *image* from the book. Multiple visualizations, representing scans of different parts of the books, can be grouped together into a collection.

The Document class is defined as [7]:

> A **Document** item represents a body of information produced as a result of an Execution, in the form of a communication medium. Multiple Document items may be grouped into a Collection.

Continuing with our Harry Potter example, the digital representation of the entire book *Harry Potter and the Chamber of Secrets* is the Document, whether this takes the form of a single PDF or some other digital format.

These core concepts in ProvONE enable us to be more specific in describing inputs and outputs: they are a more granular system for documenting entities. This granularity better manifests the relationship between retrospective and prospective provenance, between the past and future of something.

Knowing the structure and rationales behind a conceptual model are crucial first steps to gaining a comprehensive understanding of the model. Next, we want to put the model into use in a real-world context. Here, we will use a fun example, the popular Nintendo video game *Animal Crossing: New Horizons* to showcase some important classes in the data structure of ProvONE.

Fig. 4.4 Data structure classes explained in *Animal Crossing: New Horizons* example

Animal Crossing: New Horizons (ACNH) is a virtual, DIY simulation game for the Nintendo Switch gaming system. In the game, players can design their own island living environments and make tools, furniture, and seasonal decor based on recipes. The process of collecting resources and recipes to make specific items represents an opportunity to practice prospective provenance making with ProvONE.

In the winter season, *ACNH* islands get covered in a blanket of snow. Among a variety of snow- and iced-themed decor, players can make snowpersons. As in real life, making snowpersons usually comprises two stacked snowballs, and only when we get the proportions of the snowballs right are we able to come up with a "perfect" snowperson, one where the top snowball is somewhat smaller than the bottom snowball. In this sense, the final product we are aiming to make, a perfect snowperson, is an *entity*, while the ingredients to make the snowperson, the two snowballs, are the *data* (see Fig. 4.4).

Notice that in Fig. 4.5 we only render one snowball class (data:Snowball) as a subclass of entity:Snowperson instead of two snowballs. This is because the ProvONE conceptual model depicts generic classes but not instances of an entity. Using this snowperson example, we will explore the two other main constructs that ProvONE creates in addition to the data structure, *trace* and *workflow*.

Fig. 4.5 *ACNH* example: Data Structure classes in ProvONE

4.5.2 Trace: Retrospective Provenance

The trace aspect in ProvONE houses the subclasses and associations for describing the retrospective provenance of an entity. An *execution* is used as an entity (Fig. 4.1) that connects the data structure aspect to the trace aspect. Within a trace, a user made the execution at a point in time, therefore the user is associated with activities that have already happened (Fig. 4.6). Both user and execution are subclasses of the PROV classes agent and activity, respectively. Notice how the verb usage in the class and association names are all past-tense: this contrasts to how we will talk about workflows, and really indicates that traces are about what happened in the past.

ProvONE Trace classes in RDF

```
provone:Execution rdfs:subClassOf prov:Activity
provone:User rdfs:subClassOf prov:Agent
```

Let's return to the *Animal Crossing: New Horizons* example to consider a utilization of a trace in ProvONE. In *ACNH*, the snowy season lasts several months. During that time, a player could make multiple snowpersons on their island. Previously, we established that the snowperson is an entity. The activity of generating a snowperson can be modeled as an execution that realizes the entity. To put it simply, if the ProvONE user, who we'll call Emery, made 100 snowpersons, then they are associated with each of the 100 snowpersons' executions (Fig. 4.7). In ProvONE, an execution can have nested executions, connected by a many-to-many *wasInformedBy* association, or a many-to-one *wasPartOf* association

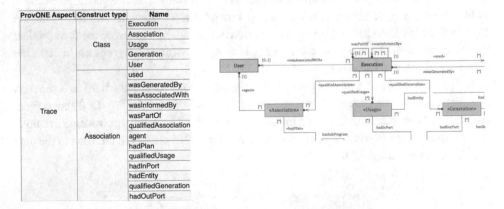

Fig. 4.6 Trace aspect in ProvONE. Left:ProvONE classes table. Right: Corresponding section in ProvONE model

Fig. 4.7 Trace classes explained in *Animal Crossing: New Horizons* example

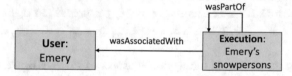

Fig. 4.8 *ACNH* example: trace classes in ProvONE

(see Fig. 4.6). Therefore, we can say that Emery's snowperson #1 (an instance of the execution) *wasPartOf* all Emery's snowpersons in winter (an abstract idea of the execution) (Fig. 4.8). Executions (what was done) can then be associated with the Program of "how to make snowpersons" (what can be done), which we will discuss in the following section.

4.5.3 Workflow: Prospective Provenance

ProvONE associates trace (or retrospective) aspects like executions with their workflow (prospective) counterparts. In other words, it connects what happened with what can or will happen (Fig. 4.9). The workflow aspect demonstrates the recipes or plans for an activity and depicts the nuances of the recipes. A *program* is the idea of a recipe and a workflow is the specific method that realizes that idea. A program can be singular or it can be composite to support nested programs via the *hasSubProgram* association. In a similar sense, a program can be realized by multiple *workflows*, just as there are many roads that lead to Rome.

In RDF, program is a subclass of both entity and plan, whereas workflow is a subclass of program.

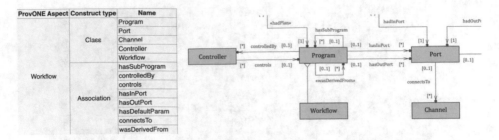

Fig. 4.9 Workflow aspect in ProvONE. Left:ProvONE classes table. Right: Corresponding section in ProvONE model

---

ProvONE Workflow classes in RDF

```
provone:Program rdfs:subClassOf prov:Entity
provone:Program rdfs:subClassOf prov:Plan
provone:Workflow rdfs:subClassOf provone:Program
```

To best explain the classes in the workflow aspect of ProvONE, we will continue our *Animal Crossing: New Horizons* example. We now know the *entity*, *data*, *user*, and *execution* of making a snowperson, but *how* do we make a "perfect" snowperson with correct size ratio between the top and bottom snowballs?

Entity	Snowperson
Data	Snowballs
User	Player emery
Execution	Snowperson #36

In this case, the *program* we want is *How to Build a Perfect Snowperson* or *Building a Perfect Snowperson*. There are many ways to build a snowperson, but in *Animal Crossing*, if we do not follow specific methods, the snowperson will not be perfect and the anthropomorphic snowperson will complain to the player about the quality of their work. There are different methods, or workflows, that help realize this program to make a perfect snowperson. Below, we illustrate three different *workflows* for accomplishing the program (Figs. 4.10 and 4.11).

1. Time method: Roll the snowballs for 10 seconds to make the perfect shape to form a perfect snowperson.
2. Tiles method: Roll the snowballs for the length of 10 tiles in order to make it into the perfect shape to form a perfect snowperson.

Fig. 4.10 Workflow classes explained in *Animal Crossing: New Horizons* example

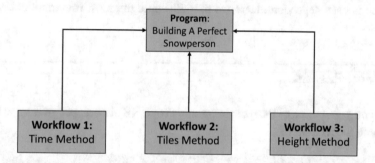

Fig. 4.11 *ACNH* example: Workflow classes in ProvONE

3. Height method: Roll the snowballs until they reach the height that match the user's earlobes to make it into the perfect shape to form a perfect snowperson.

There are other nuances within ProvONE to depict the prospective provenance of an entity. For instance, there may well be other workflows to build a perfect snowperson that are not included in Fig. 4.9. The Perfect Snowperson Program may also be comprised of *sub-programs*, such as a sub-program about *How to Find Snowballs* or *How to Generate a New Snowball When You Accidentally Ruin One*.

Notice that in Fig. 4.12 where we connect the boxes with dotted arrow lines in our ProvONE document, it looks slightly different from the actual ProvONE conceptual model. This is because some classes and associations may be optional, and the decision on which

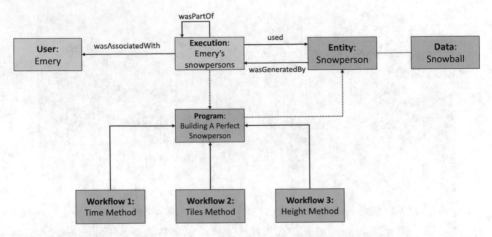

Fig. 4.12 *ACNH* example with all three ProvONE aspects combined: data structure, trace, workflow

ones to use is case-dependent. Here we only illustrate the most important classes for the *ACNH* case.

4.6 Mini-Exercise

Now that you know some of the most important ProvONE classes, put your knowledge into practice with a new example.

Our user Emery is given a new recipe to make a *Frozen Sculpture*. There are some materials needed in order to craft the sculpture. Making a Frozen Sculpture requires 1 large snowflake and 4 [regular] snowflakes. With wit and courage, Emery manages to acquire the correct materials and build their Frozen Sculpture. With the recipe in hand, Emery can make many more Frozen Sculptures in the future if they want to (see Fig. 4.13). To model this workflow, we first need to determine which ProvONE concepts to employ. In the table below, determine what entities, data, users, executions, and programs are needed to express the process of building a Frozen Sculpture.

Fig. 4.13 Can you identify the ProvONE classes Entity, Data, User, Execution, Program, and Workflow in this example?

Fill in the table:

ProvONE class	Your answer
Entity	
Data	
User	
Execution	
Program	
Workflow	

Like our examples throughout the chapter, you may first want to distinguish what the three aspects of ProvONE are in this case. What parts of this example are Data Structure? What parts are in the Trace aspect? What are in the Workflow aspect? This thought process will help you differentiate the prospective and retrospective provenance in this example. Emery followed a recipe and made a Frozen Sculpture, and using the recipe, Emery can and will make more Frozen Sculptures. For Data Structure, what are the generic classes of materials that Emery needs and used to build the Frozen Sculpture? What are the instances of the exact number of materials that Emery needs and used? For Trace, what did Emery build, or execute? For Workflow aspects, think about what this recipe is, and what are the possible different methods that can realize this recipe. For a challenge, think about the fact that before building, particular materials are required. How *did* Emery get the snowflakes in the first place? What are the tools require for obtaining the snowflakes? How will Emery find snowflakes to make new Frozen Sculptures? Does this change your answers in the table?

You may apply the same exercise to your own examples to make a ProvONE document, or you can try some other examples we mentioned earlier in this chapter or in other chapters, such as data cleaning of a dataset, or topic modeling with the text in *Harry Potter and the Chamber of Secrets*.

4.7   Summary

ProvONE is a conceptual model for describing the data structure, traces, and workflows of an activity. In this chapter, you learned about:

- ProvONE and related provenance models: P-Plan, OPMW, D-OPM
- The distinction between prospective provenance and retrospective provenance; prospective provenance is what *will* be done. Retrospective provenance is what *has been* done
- The ProvONE main classes: entity, data, user, execution, program, workflow
- How to implement ProvONE main classes in simple cases

This chapter offered a brief introduction to ProvONE. Beyond the topics discussed in this chapter, ProvONE inherits concepts and terms from workflow systems like Kepler, such as those incorporated into D-OPM, a precursor to ProvONE. ProvONE also contains constructs such as *ports* and *channels* in a program, where ports represent prospective production or consumption of data, and channels describe the flow of data between ports. Additional information and resources can be found in the ProvONE documentation. We will briefly return to ProvONE in the concluding chapter (Chap. 8) as we look at trends in provenance metadata.

References

1. Randall D, Welser C (2018) The irreproducibility crisis of modern science: causes, consequences, and the road to reform. ERIC
2. Matthew R, Merriam T (1993) Neural computation in stylometry I: an application to the works of Shakespeare and Fletcher. Lit Linguist Comput 8(4):203–209
3. Zhao Y, Zobel J (2007) Searching with style: authorship attribution in classic literature. ACM Int Conf Proc Ser 244:59–68
4. Garijo D, Gil Y (2013) The P-PLAN ontology. https://www.opmw.org/model/p-plan/. Cited 10 Mar 2022
5. Garijo D, Gil Y (2014) The OPMW-PROV ontology. https://www.opmw.org/model/OPMW/. Cited 10 Mar 2022
6. Cuevas-Vicenttín V, Dey S, Wang M, Song T, Ludascher B (2012) Modeling and querying scientific workflow provenance in the D-OPM. In: SC companion: high performance computing, networking storage and analysis. https://doi.org/10.1109/SC.Companion.2012.27
7. Cuevas-Vincenttin V, Ludascher B, Missier P, Belhajjame K, Chirigati F, Wei Y, Dey S, et al (2016) ProvONE: a PROV extension data model for scientific workflow provenance. https://purl.dataone.org/provone-v1-dev. Cited 10 Mar 2022

Introduction to PREMIS

5

5.1 Learning Objectives

The primary goal of this chapter is to introduce PREMIS, the Preservation Metadata Initiative, and outline its features as a provenance model. In this chapter, you will learn about:

- A brief history of PREMIS
- An introduction to the main PREMIS entities
- How to create simple PREMIS records

5.2 What is PREMIS?

> PREMIS' Goal: "to develop a core set of implementable preservation metadata, broadly applicable across a wide range of digital preservation contexts and supported by guidelines and recommendations for creation, management, and use." –PREMIS Editorial Committee, 2015, p. 1.

The field of digital preservation is young and actively evolving all the time. The Digital Preservation Coalition defines digital preservation as, "[...] the series of managed activities necessary to ensure continued access to digital materials for as long as necessary. Digital preservation...refers to all of the actions required to maintain access to digital materials beyond the limits of media failure or technological and organisational change" [1].

The wicked problems associated with digital preservation became apparent before the professionalization of the field began in earnest: organizations from NASA to Pixar struggled to maintain access to the digital data they generated at significant cost, with the volume of data associated with discrete projects rising quickly. Pixar famously nearly lost *Toy Story 2* when someone accidentally deleted the animation that had been in development for more than a year. A technical director working from home after giving birth had copies at her house that were saved from the purge; this fortuitous circumstance rescued the picture. The total data NASA produced with the Mars Reconnaissance Orbiter as of 2012 was 19 Terabytes, which was more than 3 times the amount of data from all prior deep space missions combined. A diverse collection of parties came together to create the first standard in digital preservation, the Open Archival Information System Reference Model (OAIS) [2]. OAIS originated with the Consultative Committee for Space Data Systems in 1999 and became an ISO standard for digital preservation in the early 2000s [3].

Concurrently, people engaged in digital preservation work recognized the need for standardized metadata to support the theoretical framework suggested by OAIS. PREMIS, which stands for *PREservation Metadata Implementation Strategies*, provides a schema that is flexible enough to be implemented anywhere digital preservation activities occur, from space and other science data to archives and e-records to private industry. In short, PREMIS is a provenance metadata schema designed to track digital preservation metadata. Unlike some analog preservation, there is no benign neglect in the world of digital preservation: at a minimum, the light and power must be on to maintain access to digital content.

5.3   PREMIS: A Brief History

PREMIS was developed as a joint effort between OCLC and RLG between 2003–2005, after a 2002 report from the OCLC/RLG Preservation Metadata Framework Working Group on OAIS and preservation metadata [4].

PREMIS materials are currently maintained by the Library of Congress and PREMIS undergoes continual revision by an editorial committee. Its development history is illustrative of the evolution of standards in heavy use (Table 5.1): PREMIS has been adapted and updated over the years to meet the needs of practitioners in its domain space, digital preservation. PREMIS has become the *de facto* international standard for digital preservation metadata, used in institutions around the world [5]. The Library of Congress' PREMIS page includes materials in Czech, English, German, Italian, Portuguese, and Spanish. This widespread use has led to the incorporation of PREMIS into commercial and open-source content man-

Table 5.1 PREMIS timeline

PREMIS development timeline	
Version 1.0	2005
Version 2.0	2008
Revisions	2011
Revisions	2012
Version 3.0	2015
Release of 3.0 Schema	2016

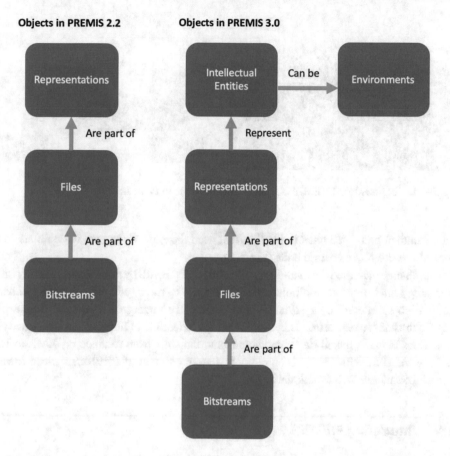

Fig. 5.1 Change in object model in PREMIS from version 2.2 to 3.0

agement, repository, and digital preservation tools. There have been many smaller changes to PREMIS over the years, like distinguishing between checksums and message digests or applying storage information semantic units to bitstreams that previously only applied to files.[1] Other changes have been larger, impacting the foundational data model of itself. One of the largest changes was the reallocation of computational environment information in version 3.0 (Fig. 5.1).

In version 2.2, information about the hardware and software necessary to render a file (*environment information*) was contained inside individual file entities. The structural shift that occurred in the change to version 3.0 took that environment information out of the file record and placed it in its own record. Environment information could now be expressed separately as its own related stack of objects for software and hardware. This information

---

[1] https://www.loc.gov/standards/premis/changes-v2-0.html.

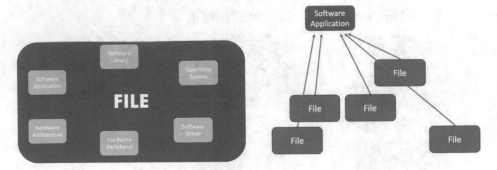

Fig. 5.2 Environments in PREMIS 2.2 versus environments in PREMIS 3.0

stack can then be related back to the files that need those environments via pointers in the form of *relationship* semantic units (Fig. 5.2).

This change increased the modularity of records in PREMIS by allowing users to construct technology environments and point multiple objects to them, without the need to change multiple object records every time a software program undergoes a version change (Fig. 5.2). Such changes reflect trends in the technology landscape in libraries, archives, and data collections towards linked data applications and the shift from reliance on XML to RDF dominance. The PREMIS OWL ontology is an embodiment of PREMIS's move towards potential Semantic Web functionality [6].

5.4   Modeling PREMIS

PREMIS' top-level entities enable preservationists to document the histories of the digital objects that will grow in time as on-going preservation work takes place: how those objects came to be, at various points of time in their lifecycle. A single digital object record can point to a snowballing series of events as the object is ingested, stored, updated, and shared, updated and shared again, updated and shared again...iteratively. The retrospective provenance will grow over time. In addition to creating records for the provenance of digital objects, PREMIS also contains structures for documenting a functional computing environment for the digital objects; the people, organizations, and software making preservation decisions; and relevant intellectual property rights for the objects themselves and the associated software (Fig. 5.3).

5.4.1   PREMIS Semantic Units

PREMIS is made up of a set of *semantic units* that are meant to be more adaptable than traditional fixed metadata elements, in recognition of the broad spectrum of institutions doing digital preservation work. PREMIS uses the term *semantic units* rather than the common

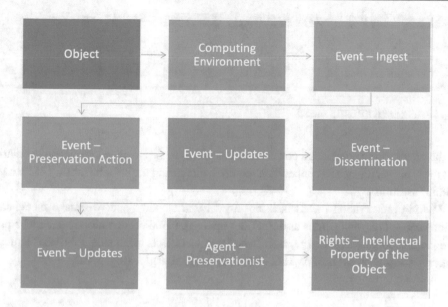

Fig. 5.3 Tracking digital object provenance

metadata term *elements* because metadata elements imply a specific way of encoding a record or a database. Because PREMIS can be used in so many situations and systems, it may not show up encoded as metadata or in a database, in which case its organizing structure represents a set of semantic units, or simply put, defined pieces of information [7].

Importantly, PREMIS functions as a 'core' standard. This means that PREMIS does not cover all eventualities with specificity, but rather covers only those things that most institutions need to know most of the time [7]. Filling in a PREMIS record requires a careful appraisal of provenance data: selecting those most crucial bits for a record, and leaving other things out. This means that areas such as descriptive, technical, and personnel-related metadata are brief in PREMIS' semantic units, with the opportunity to add additional content in extension containers or to have additional records elsewhere in other formats. For example, a more detailed description of archival content might exist in digital finding aid; the HR department might have more information on the agents involved in preservation actions like reformatting and storage; you might embed a full record from a technical schema with specific format details into an extension unit within PREMIS; or PREMIS can be bundled together with a number of additional records within a structural metadata schema like METS.[2]

The semantic units within PREMIS touch on basic descriptive, technical, and other administrative metadata. They also provide a structure to document preservation-specific provenance information like the methods of preservation employed by an institution or records

---

[2] METS: https://www.loc.gov/standards/mets/.

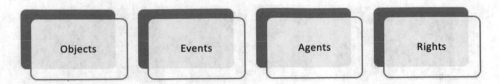

Fig. 5.4 A partial PREMIS model

of the preservation processes a conservator has taken. It uses many controlled vocabularies, but these are recommended rather than required, increasing the customizability of PREMIS within institutions.

Making preservation metadata is not a goal that stands alone: we make metadata in furtherance of our obligations as digital stewards [8]. Good preservation metadata helps us to document, organize, preserve, and disseminate the objects in our care. PREMIS' structure features 4 top-level entities: *objects*, *events*, *agents*, and *rights* (Fig. 5.4).

5.4.2   Objects

PREMIS focuses predominantly on objects, which are the preservation targets or the things we actually want to preserve. They are the most important entities in a PREMIS record; events, agents, and rights play supporting roles. Therefore, there is the capacity within PREMIS to do the most detailed information work in relation to these objects. Objects can be further broken down into 4 categories:

- Intellectual Entities
- Representations
- Files
- Bitstreams

A **bitstream** object documents a string of ones and zeros that do not stand alone as an entire file. This could represent part of a file, for example just the PCM portion of a WAV file.[3] It could represent the 1s and 0s of a virus that has infected a file.

A **file** object is relatively self-explanatory and offers the most room for technical specificity. Files are recognizable by software and operating systems. For files, PREMIS requires the documentation of format information. It also gives room to note information like size, fixity, creating software, and alternate names, among other semantic units. A file could contain PREMIS-documented bitstreams, but it does not have to.

A **representation** object has two functions within the PREMIS model. First, it operates in later versions as a place to document physical objects that are crucial to the preservation

---

[3] https://en.wikipedia.org/wiki/WAV.

of digital content. While PREMIS is designed for the provenance of digital content, many digital objects are inseparable from related analog components. When preserving digitized content, it can be important to note the analog object from which the digital objects were derived. For example, in preserving video games like the 1985 *Carmen Sandiego* PC game, it is necessary to track the analog paperback encyclopedia that came bundled with the floppy disk, because that specific book acts as copy protection necessary to play the game. In such cases, representations can be used to store information about these physical objects. The required semantic units for representation objects are different than those for file objects, which makes sense: a file has a size in bytes, whereas a paperback book does not.

Second, representation objects can also serve as a semantic unit to document sets of files that work together. An example could be something like a digitized book: each page of the book is scanned, producing OCR files. Every individual OCR file would have a file object; the set of file objects altogether that make up the totality of the book would be a representation object.

Intellectual entity objects are the most complicated because of the myriad different potential purposes they can serve in a PREMIS record. If bitstreams can make up files, and files can make up representations, multiple representations can represent intellectual entities. Intellectual entity objects can serve to logically tie together several other objects. In this way, they can function like a collection. In a similar vein, **intellectual entity objects** can serve to document a larger idea or work represented by representation and file objects. In this case, intellectual entities are akin to FRBR works, with the representations and files functioning as manifestations and items [9].

The complexity with intellectual entities comes from the fact that, outside the stack that makes up a single conceptual object [10], they are also used as containers to document rendering environments for digital content (see Fig. 5.2 on environments). We can document software applications, software libraries, operating systems, and hardware as a series of related **intellectual entity objects**. The distinction between FRBR work intellectual entities and environment intellectual entities is made clear in the use of the *semantic subunits*, semantic units nested hierarchically within other semantic units. While a FRBR work might have a name, a significant property, and some related representations and files, an environment has controlled vocabularies for environment types, software types, hardware types, and subunits to name and version software programs. In previous versions of PREMIS, intellectual entities stood alone; as of version 3, they became the fourth type of object [11].

Once we break down PREMIS objects in 4 categories, we can expand our PREMIS model to incorporate these categories along with the different functions of representations and intellectual entities (Fig. 5.5).

Within a PREMIS record, we can connect different discrete sections with different semantic units. We can connect objects to other objects using relationships. Relationships can tie together different parts of an environment together, like the Pages software application to a Mac Big Sur operating system. Relationships can also tie digital objects together, to show that a jpeg file is derived from a tiff file or to show that a series of file objects comprise a rep-

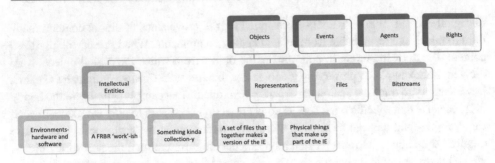

Fig. 5.5 A full PREMIS model

Table 5.2 Relationship type controlled vocabulary scheme members

Scheme members
Dependency
Derivation
Logical
Reference
Replacement
Structural

resentation object set. These relationships have both types and subtypes, with recommended controlled vocabularies hosted by the Library of Congress (Table 5.2).[4]

We can also connect the top-level entities with linking semantic units. These are not typed, but they can be bi- or uni-directional. Links can connect

- Objects to events (things happening to the object) or rights (the IP for the object)
- Events to agents (who is doing the thing) or objects
- Agents to rights (who owns the rights) or events
- Rights to agents or objects

Using PREMIS, a single XML file can contain the ever-living history of a digital object. The object itself is described by a file object. Its history in the institution is documented through a series of events, each of which points back to the object. A set of agents points to the events they had a hand in doing. And the rights to the file tie an object to the person or corporation who owns the relevant IP. Inter-object relationships tell us which software and hardware are necessary to display and use the file. These records can be simple: the required semantic units are few. At the same time, there is both flexibility and extensibility to document great detail about the provenance of digital objects in PREMIS. In the next

---

[4] https://id.loc.gov/vocabulary/preservation/relationshipType.html.

section of this chapter, we will make a sample record for some digital content in order to gain some familiarity with PREMIS.

5.4.3 Mini-Exercise: Objects

In this section, we will explore some basic PREMIS making. In this use case, our test object is a short video of a child playing with a piece of interactive sculpture art. To begin with, the table provides some basic technical information about the digital video obtained using version 6.5 of the DROID file format identification tool (Table 5.3).

We will start the record with the central concern of PREMIS, the digital object for which we want to record provenance. In order to build this record, we will make extensive use of the PREMIS Data Dictionary,[5] which explains the development process of the standard, lays out all the semantic units in order, and links to the various PREMIS controlled vocabularies [5].

The Data Dictionary lays out the semantic units, the order in which they should or must appear, and which units are required. For example, the Data Dictionary starts with unit 1.1 objectIdentifier. The objectIdentifier unit is labeled both M and R, or mandatory and repeatable. This tells us that within PREMIS, this identifier information must be the first part of the record, and that we may store multiple identifiers. Unit 1.3 preservationLevel is labeled as both O and R, or optional and repeatable. A file might have multiple preservationLevels associated with it, or none. Additionally, unit 1.3 preservationLevel is also labeled with [Intellectual Entity, Representation, File], which means that this unit can apply to those 3 classes of objects and that the fourth class, bitstreams, cannot use the preservationLevel semantic units. The data dictionary also provides explanations and examples for each semantic unit.

Table 5.3 DROID file identification tool output for sample file

DROID output	
Resource	file:///Users/username/Files/PoP/SampleVideo.mov
Extension	mov
Size	12042168
Last modified	7/12/21, 10:58 AM
Format	Quicktime
MIME type	Video/quicktime
PRONOM unique ID (PUID)	x-fmt/384
MD5 signature	151e4e5a49f462ec673a707c30a20361

---

[5] https://www.loc.gov/standards/premis/v3/premis-3-0-final.pdf.

Table 5.4 DROID file Identifier

Semantic unit	Value
1.1.1 IdentifierType	Filepath
1.1.2 IdentifierValue	file:///Users/username/Files/PoP/SampleVideo.mov

Each section of a PREMIS record begins with identity information. These identifiers are crucial in that they allow us to associate different portions of the records as it grows over an object's lifetime. Many segments can be recorded within a single XML file, and only certain segments will relate directly to one another. PREMIS offers a suggested, but not mandatory, list of identifier types. In this case, we can identify our file using the information in the DROID output (Table 5.4).

Using the data dictionary as a guide, fill in values for the following semantic units using the DROID output for the SampleVideo in the chart below. Answers can be found in the supplementary materials (metaprov.org).

Semantic unit	Value
1.5.2.1 messageDigestAlgorithm	
1.5.2.2 messageDigest	
1.5.2.3 messageDigestOriginator	
1.5.3 size	
1.5.4.1.1 formatName	
1.5.4.2.1 formatRegistryName	
1.5.4.2.2 formatRegistryKey	

These two tables combined contain the basic data necessary for a very simple PREMIS record for the SampleVideo file. We could stop now and enter the information into an XML document, and it would validate against the PREMIS schema .xsd hosted by the Library of Congress (Fig. 5.6).

This record, however, is not great for documenting the provenance of the object in the longer term. It does provide structure for some crucial existential information about the SampleVideo file: it notes that these particular 1s and 0s comprise a file, how big the file is, and what kind of file it is. It also provides fixity information that allows a digital steward to ensure the integrity of the file does not change over time. But it does not document very much provenance. To do so, some additions must be made:

1. We can add additional optional semantic units within the <PREMIS:object> space to document more about the origins and significant properties of the object. These units include things like significant property wrappers, creating software program information, the file's original name, and storage information about the file.

2. We can also add some institutional policy metadata by using the preservation level semantic units within the <PREMIS:object>. These allow us to note whether digital preservation actions should focus on maintaining several back-up copies of the original 1s and 0s or whether some full or logical preservation of the object, which might involve the creation of new 1s and 0s in the form of migration copies, makes more sense for the collection and collecting institution.

These options can be explored in greater detail by reading through the Object-specific semantic units in the PREMIS Data Dictionary.

5.4.4 Events

We can also expand this record by adding additional sections to it, like event, agent, and rights information. Event and agent sections of a record are very simple, in their role as supporting evidence for the object being preserved. They require a minimal number of semantic units to validate, focusing mostly on identifiers. However, the flexibility of PREMIS does enable

```xml
<?xml version="1.0" encoding="UTF-8"?>
<PREMIS:premis xmlns:PREMIS="http://www.loc.gov/premis/v3"
    xmlns:xsi="http://www.w3.org/2001/XMLSchema-instance"
    xsi:schemaLocation="http://www.loc.gov/premis/v3
    https://www.loc.gov/standards/premis/v3/premis-v3-0.xsd"
    version="3.0">
    <PREMIS:object xsi:type="PREMIS:file">
        <PREMIS:objectIdentifier>
            <PREMIS:objectIdentifierType>filepath</PREMIS:objectIdentifierType>
            <PREMIS:objectIdentifierValue>file:///Users/username/Files/PoP/SampleVideo.mov
            </PREMIS:objectIdentifierValue>
        </PREMIS:objectIdentifier>
        <PREMIS:objectCharacteristics>
            <PREMIS:fixity>
                <PREMIS:messageDigestAlgorithm>MD5</PREMIS:messageDigestAlgorithm>
                <PREMIS:messageDigest>151e4e5a49f462ec673a707c30a20361</PREMIS:messageDigest>
                <PREMIS:messageDigestOriginator>DROID</PREMIS:messageDigestOriginator>
            </PREMIS:fixity>
            <PREMIS:size>12042168</PREMIS:size>
            <PREMIS:format>
                <PREMIS:formatDesignation>
                    <PREMIS:formatName>Quicktime</PREMIS:formatName>
                </PREMIS:formatDesignation>
                <PREMIS:formatRegistry>
                    <PREMIS:formatRegistryName>Pronom</PREMIS:formatRegistryName>
                    <PREMIS:formatRegistryKey>x-fmt/384</PREMIS:formatRegistryKey>
                </PREMIS:formatRegistry>
            </PREMIS:format>
        </PREMIS:objectCharacteristics>
    </PREMIS:object>
```

Fig. 5.6 Validating XML for the sample video

more expansive documentation where appropriate. PREMIS events aim to capture the history of the object being preserved. It primarily provides structure to document what is happening to your objects; through links, it allows you to specify who is doing these things and what objects they are doing them to. The PREMIS Data Dictionary links to an extensive controlled vocabulary of possible event types (Fig. 5.7).

In addition to eventType, PREMIS has semantic units for the date and time of the event; free text fields for details; and outcome information. Events can also be linked to the agents who did them and the objects they happened to.

5.4.5   Agents

Agents are similarly brief in their semantic units. Agents have a typology as well, but it is rather simpler. Similar to agents in PROV, PREMIS agents can be a *person*, an *organization*, a *software*, or a *hardware*. This is because agents cover both the entities that do something or compel something to happen as well as rights holders. In addition to people as agents, software may have an agency role in the workflow of events that happen to a digital object: a content management system may be set up to independently run fixity checks or virus scans; digital preservation software may automatically generate metadata records. Organizations, such as software companies, or large-scale rights holders, like a publishing or record company, may own the intellectual property associated with the preservation objects or aspects of their computing environments.

Beyond the type, agent semantic units allow for the documentation of the agent's name and its version, if it is a software agent. Two additional units allow for more expansive information about agents: agentNote units are free text units designed to hold additional information to further disambiguate or define an agent; agentExtension units function as containers to embed external content, such as other metadata records from other schemas, for example, FOAF information about a person.

5.4.6   Mini-Exercise: Event and Agent

Let us return to the Sample Video file. Here, we will make a simple **event** and **agent** record to link to the object information we documented earlier. Fill out the skeletal event record for the SampleVideo. Using the eventType controlled vocabulary displayed in Fig. 5.7, decide what kind of event might be appropriate for the SampleVideo based on the DROID output. You can source date material from the DROID output or make up appropriate date material. Remember that the PREMIS Data Dictionary provides examples and links to controlled vocabularies as well as information regarding the formatting of things like times and dates. You should also take the object identifier information from the earlier part of this

Fig. 5.7 Event type controlled vocabulary for PREMIS (https://id.loc.gov/vocabulary/preservation/eventType.html)

- Accession
- Appraisal
- Capture
- Compression
- Creation
- Deaccession
- Decompression
- Decryption
- Deletion
- Digital signature generation
- Digital signature validation
- Dissemination
- Encryption
- Filename change
- Fixity check
- Forensic feature analysis
- Format identification
- Imaging
- Information package creation
- Information package merging
- Information package splitting
- Ingestion
- Ingestion end
- Ingestion start
- Message digest calculation
- Metadata extraction
- Metadata modification
- Migration
- Modification
- Normalization
- Packing
- Policy assignment
- Quarantine
- Recovery
- Redaction
- Refreshment
- Replication
- Transfer
- Unpacking
- Unquarantine
- Validation
- Virus check

exercise. Once you have filled in the information for an event, fill in information for the agent responsible for this event.

Element	Value
2.1.1 eventIdentifierType	LocallyDefinedIdentifier
2.1.2 eventIdentifierValue	Event1
2.2 eventType	
2.3 eventDateTime	
2.6.1 linkingAgentIdentifierType	
2.6.2 linkingAgentIdentifierValue	
2.6.3 linkingAgentRole	
2.7.1 linkingObjectIdentifierType	
2.7.2 linkingObjectIdentifierValue	
3.1.1 agentIdentifierType	LocallyDefinedIdentifier
3.1.2 agentIdentifierValue	Agent1
3.2 agentName	
3.3 agentType	
3.7.1 linkingEventIdentifierType	
3.7.2 linkingEventIdentifierValue	

We can add this information to our previous object information. The event and agent information provide a kernel of provenance metadata about the digital object in the form of dated information describing some history for the object and the people, organizations, or technology involved in the history. This information would be contained within the same, continuous XML document (Fig. 5.8):

```
<PREMIS:event>
    <PREMIS:eventIdentifier>
        <PREMIS:eventIdentifierType>locallyDefinedIdentifier</PREMIS:eventIdentifierType>
        <PREMIS:eventIdentifierValue>Event1</PREMIS:eventIdentifierValue>
    </PREMIS:eventIdentifier>
    <PREMIS:eventType>modification</PREMIS:eventType>
    <PREMIS:eventDateTime>2021-07-21T10:58</PREMIS:eventDateTime>
    <PREMIS:linkingAgentIdentifier>
        <PREMIS:linkingAgentIdentifierType>locallyDefinedIdentifier
        </PREMIS:linkingAgentIdentifierType>
        <PREMIS:linkingAgentIdentifierValue>Agent1</PREMIS:linkingAgentIdentifierValue>
        <PREMIS:linkingAgentRole>implementor</PREMIS:linkingAgentRole>
    </PREMIS:linkingAgentIdentifier>
    <PREMIS:linkingObjectIdentifier>
        <PREMIS:linkingObjectIdentifierType>filepath</PREMIS:linkingObjectIdentifierType>
        <PREMIS:linkingObjectIdentifierValue>file:///Users/username/Files/PoP/SampleVideo.mov
        </PREMIS:linkingObjectIdentifierValue>
    </PREMIS:linkingObjectIdentifier>
</PREMIS:event>

<PREMIS:agent>
    <PREMIS:agentIdentifier>
        <PREMIS:agentIdentifierType>locallyDefinedIdentifier</PREMIS:agentIdentifierType>
        <PREMIS:agentIdentifierValue>Agent1</PREMIS:agentIdentifierValue>
    </PREMIS:agentIdentifier>
    <PREMIS:agentName>Hay Jent</PREMIS:agentName>
    <PREMIS:agentType>person</PREMIS:agentType>
    <PREMIS:linkingEventIdentifier>
        <PREMIS:linkingEventIdentifierType>locallyDefinedIdentifier
        </PREMIS:linkingEventIdentifierType>
        <PREMIS:linkingEventIdentifierValue>Event1</PREMIS:linkingEventIdentifierValue>
    </PREMIS:linkingEventIdentifier>
</PREMIS:agent>
```

Fig. 5.8 XML document for this exercise

We now have an event and an agent that *link* to each other. The event also links back to the digital objects in question, the SampleVideo file. At this point we can extend our initial object information to link to the event we have created (Fig. 5.9).

5.4.7   Rights

The fourth major entity in a PREMIS record is a rights section. Rights in PREMIS are predominantly focused on intellectual property (IP) such as copyright status and license information. Rights information in PREMIS will apply to the digital objects documented as representations, files, and bitstreams; it is also frequently necessary for software used as part of computing environments known to work with the digital objects. Legal situations surrounding digital objects can be complicated, especially when dealing with objects that contain layers of materials with different rights holders, like a film with image rights, trade-marked brands, and popular music soundtracks. Orphan works and abandonware also pose challenges in determining the rights status of materials in digital data and collections.

When making PREMIS rights statements, institutions can lean on rights work done by organizations such as Creative Commons and righsstatements.org to provide succinct,

```
<PREMIS:object xsi:type="PREMIS:file">
    <PREMIS:objectIdentifier>
        <PREMIS:objectIdentifierType>filepath</PREMIS:objectIdentifierType>
        <PREMIS:objectIdentifierValue>file:///Users/username/Files/PoP/SampleVideo.mov
        </PREMIS:objectIdentifierValue>
    </PREMIS:objectIdentifier>
    <PREMIS:objectCharacteristics>
        <PREMIS:fixity>
            <PREMIS:messageDigestAlgorithm>MD5</PREMIS:messageDigestAlgorithm>
            <PREMIS:messageDigest>151e4e5a49f462ec673a707c30a20361</PREMIS:messageDigest>
            <PREMIS:messageDigestOriginator>DROID</PREMIS:messageDigestOriginator>
        </PREMIS:fixity>
        <PREMIS:size>12042168</PREMIS:size>
        <PREMIS:format>
            <PREMIS:formatDesignation>
                <PREMIS:formatName>Quicktime</PREMIS:formatName>
            </PREMIS:formatDesignation>
            <PREMIS:formatRegistry>
                <PREMIS:formatRegistryName>Pronom</PREMIS:formatRegistryName>
                <PREMIS:formatRegistryKey>x-fmt/384</PREMIS:formatRegistryKey>
            </PREMIS:formatRegistry>
        </PREMIS:format>
    </PREMIS:objectCharacteristics>
    <PREMIS:linkingEventIdentifier>
        <PREMIS:linkingEventIdentifierType>locallyDefinedIdentifier
        </PREMIS:linkingEventIdentifierType>
        <PREMIS:linkingEventIdentifierValue>Event1</PREMIS:linkingEventIdentifierValue>
    </PREMIS:linkingEventIdentifier>
</PREMIS:object>
```

Fig. 5.9 XML document for this exercise-continued

standardized language about the rights related to digital objects. It is also important to remember the function of PREMIS when making rights statements: PREMIS is focused primarily on digital preservation. It is a core metadata schema, aimed at documenting what most preservationists would need to know most of the time.

This means that it may not be appropriate to include a lengthy license agreement in full or a donor contract in the PREMIS record. While both are certainly possible, PREMIS is more concerned with the preservation implications of an object's IP status: can the preservationist make copies of a work? Distribute a work via an online platform? Migrate a work to an updated or entirely new format? Rights statements in PREMIS have semantic units specifically designed to document allowable actions, in addition to important yet optional elements about the date and jurisdiction of the object's IP.

5.4.8   Mini-Exercise: Rights

For the SampleVideo record as it exists thus far, there are two sets of rights an institution would want to document. Firstly, the rights to the SampleVideo itself. In July of 2021, the rights holder, the author Rhiannon Bettivia, licensed this video under the Creative Commons

BY-NC-SA license. Fill out the following chart with license information for the SampleV-
ideo:

4.1.1.1 rightsStatementIdentifierType	LocallyDefinedIdentifier
4.1.1.2 rightsStatementIdentifierValue	R1
4.1.2 rightsBasis	
4.1.4.1.1 licenseDocumentationIdentifierType	URL
4.1.4.1.2 licenseDocumentationIdentifierValue	[put the link to the appropriate CC license]
4.1.4.2 licenseTerms	
4.1.4.4.1 startDate	
4.1.7.1 rightsGranted act	
4.1.8.1 linkingObjectIdentifierType	
4.1.8.2 linkingObjectIdentifierValue	
4.1.9.1 linkingAgentIdentifierType	Orchid ID
4.1.9.2 linkingAgentIdentifierValue	0000-0003-4593-562X
4.1.9.3 linkingAgentRole	Rightsholder

This chart, in XML would look like (Fig. 5.10).

In this case, we have to add a new agent, the rights holder for the SampleVideo file (Fig. 5.11).

We can also add a rights link to the object entity at the outset of the record (Fig. 5.12).

There are other associated rights that can be included in a PREMIS record, including rights and license information for software. In this case, we could include the rights for DROID software, or software used to view the video file, such as QuickTime, and an operating system that enables the software to run. For the last part of this hands-on activity, we will make a second object record, this time an intellectual entity to denote environment information. This concept will be discussed further in Chap. 6. In this case, we will make a simple environment record for the DROID program that was used to provide technical information about the SampleVideo file.

In XML, the environment object would look like (Fig. 5.13):

Object Identifier Type	LocallyDefinedIdentifier
Object Identifier Value	Environment1
Object Category	Intellectual entity
1.9.1 environmentFunctionType	
1.9.2 environmentFunctionLevel	1
1.9.1 environmentFunctionType	
1.9.2 environmentFunctionLevel	2
1.10.1 environmentName	
1.10.2 environmentVersion	

```
<PREMIS:rights>
  <PREMIS:rightsStatement>
    <PREMIS:rightsStatementIdentifier>
      <PREMIS:rightsStatementIdentifierType>locallyDefinedIdentifier
      </PREMIS:rightsStatementIdentifierType>
      <PREMIS:rightsStatementIdentifierValue>Rights1</PREMIS:rightsStatementIdentifierValue>
    </PREMIS:rightsStatementIdentifier>
    <PREMIS:rightsBasis>license</PREMIS:rightsBasis>
    <PREMIS:licenseInformation>
      <PREMIS:licenseDocumentationIdentifier>
        <PREMIS:licenseDocumentationIdentifierType>URL
        </PREMIS:licenseDocumentationIdentifierType>
        <PREMIS:licenseDocumentationIdentifierValue>
            https://creativecommons.org/licenses/by-nc-sa/4.0/
        </PREMIS:licenseDocumentationIdentifierValue>
      </PREMIS:licenseDocumentationIdentifier>
      <PREMIS:licenseTerms>CC BY-NC-SA includes the
          following elements: credit must be given to the creator; only noncommercial uses
          of the work are permitted; adaptations must be shared under the same terms
      </PREMIS:licenseTerms>
      <PREMIS:licenseApplicableDates>
          <PREMIS:startDate>2021-07</PREMIS:startDate>
      </PREMIS:licenseApplicableDates>
    </PREMIS:licenseInformation>
    <PREMIS:rightsGranted>
      <PREMIS:act>distribute, remix, adapt, and build upon the material</PREMIS:act>
    </PREMIS:rightsGranted>
    <PREMIS:linkingObjectIdentifier>
      <PREMIS:linkingObjectIdentifierType>Filepath</PREMIS:linkingObjectIdentifierType>
      <PREMIS:linkingObjectIdentifierValue>file:///Users/username/Files/PoP/SampleVideo.mov
      </PREMIS:linkingObjectIdentifierValue>
    </PREMIS:linkingObjectIdentifier>
    <PREMIS:linkingAgentIdentifier>
      <PREMIS:linkingAgentIdentifierType>Orchid ID</PREMIS:linkingAgentIdentifierType>
      <PREMIS:linkingAgentIdentifierValue>0000-0003-4593-562X</PREMIS:linkingAgentIdentifierValue>
      <PREMIS:linkingAgentRole>rightsholder</PREMIS:linkingAgentRole>
    </PREMIS:linkingAgentIdentifier>
  </PREMIS:rightsStatement>
</PREMIS:rights>
```

Fig. 5.10 XML document for Rights mini Exercise-1

```
<PREMIS:agent>
    <PREMIS:agentIdentifier>
        <PREMIS:agentIdentifierType>Orchid ID</PREMIS:agentIdentifierType>
        <PREMIS:agentIdentifierValue>0000-0003-4593-562X</PREMIS:agentIdentifierValue>
    </PREMIS:agentIdentifier>
    <PREMIS:agentName>Rhiannon Bettivia</PREMIS:agentName>
    <PREMIS:agentType>person</PREMIS:agentType>
    <PREMIS:linkingRightsStatementIdentifier>
        <PREMIS:linkingRightsStatementIdentifierType>locallyDefinedIdentifier
        </PREMIS:linkingRightsStatementIdentifierType>
        <PREMIS:linkingRightsStatementIdentifierValue>Rights1
        </PREMIS:linkingRightsStatementIdentifierValue>
    </PREMIS:linkingRightsStatementIdentifier>
</PREMIS:agent>
```

Fig. 5.11 XML document for Rights mini Exercise-2

```
<PREMIS:object xsi:type="PREMIS:file">
    <PREMIS:objectIdentifier>
        <PREMIS:objectIdentifierType>Filepath</PREMIS:objectIdentifierType>
        <PREMIS:objectIdentifierValue>file:///Users/username/Files/PoP/SampleVideo.mov
        </PREMIS:objectIdentifierValue>
    </PREMIS:objectIdentifier>
    <PREMIS:objectCharacteristics>
        <PREMIS:fixity>
            <PREMIS:messageDigestAlgorithm>MD5</PREMIS:messageDigestAlgorithm>
            <PREMIS:messageDigest>151e4e5a49f462ec673a707c30a20361</PREMIS:messageDigest>
            <PREMIS:messageDigestOriginator>DROID</PREMIS:messageDigestOriginator>
        </PREMIS:fixity>
        <PREMIS:size>12042168</PREMIS:size>
        <PREMIS:format>
            <PREMIS:formatDesignation>
                <PREMIS:formatName>QuickTime</PREMIS:formatName>
            </PREMIS:formatDesignation>
            <PREMIS:formatRegistry>
                <PREMIS:formatRegistryName>PRONOM</PREMIS:formatRegistryName>
                <PREMIS:formatRegistryKey>x-fmt/384</PREMIS:formatRegistryKey>
            </PREMIS:formatRegistry>
        </PREMIS:format>
    </PREMIS:objectCharacteristics>
    <PREMIS:linkingEventIdentifier>
        <PREMIS:linkingEventIdentifierType>locallyDefinedIdentifier</PREMIS:linkingEventIdentifierType>
        <PREMIS:linkingEventIdentifierValue>Event1</PREMIS:linkingEventIdentifierValue>
    </PREMIS:linkingEventIdentifier>
    <PREMIS:linkingRightsStatementIdentifier>
        <PREMIS:linkingRightsStatementIdentifierType>locallyDefinedIdentifier
        </PREMIS:linkingRightsStatementIdentifierType>
        <PREMIS:linkingRightsStatementIdentifierValue>Rights1</PREMIS:linkingRightsStatementIdentifierValue>
    </PREMIS:linkingRightsStatementIdentifier>
</PREMIS:object>
```

Fig. 5.12 XML document for Rights mini Exercise-3

```
<PREMIS:object xsi:type="PREMIS:intellectualEntity">
    <PREMIS:objectIdentifier>
        <PREMIS:objectIdentifierType>locallyDefinedIdentifier</PREMIS:objectIdentifierType>
        <PREMIS:objectIdentifierValue>Environment1</PREMIS:objectIdentifierValue>
    </PREMIS:objectIdentifier>
    <PREMIS:environmentFunction>
        <PREMIS:environmentFunctionType>software</PREMIS:environmentFunctionType>
        <PREMIS:environmentFunctionLevel>1</PREMIS:environmentFunctionLevel>
    </PREMIS:environmentFunction>
    <PREMIS:environmentFunction>
        <PREMIS:environmentFunctionType>software application</PREMIS:environmentFunctionType>
        <PREMIS:environmentFunctionLevel>2</PREMIS:environmentFunctionLevel>
    </PREMIS:environmentFunction>
    <PREMIS:environmentDesignation>
        <PREMIS:environmentName>DROID</PREMIS:environmentName>
        <PREMIS:environmentVersion>6.5</PREMIS:environmentVersion>
    </PREMIS:environmentDesignation>
</PREMIS:object>
```

Fig. 5.13 XML document for the environment object

5.5   Conclusion

This chapter provided an introduction to the PREMIS digital preservation metadata standard, a provenance schema for documenting the evolving histories of digital objects. We covered:

- The history of PREMIS
- The top-level entities that make up PREMIS: objects, events, agents, and rights
- How to create simple PREMIS records

PREMIS' semantic units allow the flexibility to document the provenance of digital objects in a variety of different institutions that engage in digital stewardship work, ranging from GLAMs (galleries, libraries, archives, and museums) to eScience to industry spaces. We explored the creation of a basic PREMIS record for a single digital file. Records can be very simple, with just a few elements to describe the format of a file, and a few lines of information to describe events, agents, and rights associated with the digital file.

However, the relationship and extension features mean that records can be considerably more complex, including multiple related objects, extensive computing environments, and rights information for a number of software programs. Additionally, the long list of event types suggests there is semantic richness in describing the history of objects from creation to reformatting, to reuse, and to remixing–in other words, there is room to document detailed digital provenance.

In Chap. 7, we will explore this idea in detail using a case study from the field of nuclear magnetic resonance (NMR) spectroscopy. PREMIS records can themselves form parts of larger records. In practice, PREMIS can form a part of METS records where the provenance information is coupled with more detailed descriptive and administrative records from other metadata standards and/or homegrown metadata schemas.

Additional resources on PREMIS can be found on the Library of Congress's PREMIS homepage.[6] The page houses considerable documentation on basic PREMIS usage, including video webinars, slide decks, and numerous examples of PREMIS records for different digital objects in the various versions of PREMIS. See the supplemental materials (found at metaprov.org) for the XML documents mentioned in this chapter.

References

1. Digital Preservation Coalition (2015) Digital preservation handbook, 2nd edn. https://www. dpconline.org/handbook. Cited 10 Mar 2022
2. Lee C (2005) Defining digital preservation work: a case study of the development of the reference model for an open archival information system. University of Michigan
3. CCSDS C (2012) Reference model for an open archival information system. Consultative Committee For Space Data Systems
4. OCLC/RLG Working Group on Preservation Metadata (2002) Preservation metadata and theOAIS information model: a metadata framework to support the preservation of digital objects. http://www.oclc.org/content/dam/research/activities/pmwg/pm_framework.pdf. Cited 10 Mar 2022
5. PREMIS Editorial Committee (2015) PREMIS data dictionary for preservation metadata. version 3.0. In: Library of congress. https://www.loc.gov/standards/premis/v3/premis-3-0-final.pdf. Cited 10 Mar 2022
6. Coppens S, Peyrard S, Guenther R, Ford K, Creighton T (2011) PREMIS OWL: introduction, implementation guidelines and best practices. http://premisontologypublic.pbworks.com/w/file/46122397/PREMIS%20OWL.pdf. Cited 10 Mar 2022

---

[6] https://www.loc.gov/standards/premis/.

7. Caplan P (2009) Understanding PREMIS. Library of Congress
8. Peyrard S, Dappert A, Guenther R (2016) How to develop a digital preservation metadata profile: risk and requirements analysis. In: Dappert A, Guenther R, Peyrard S (eds) Digital preservation metadata for practitioners. Springer, Berlin. https://doi.org/10.1007/978-3-319-43763-7_17
9. Coyle K (2015) FRBR, before and after: a look at our bibliographic models. American Library Association, Chicago
10. Thibodeau K (2002) Overview of technological approaches to digital preservation and challenges in coming years. Council on Library and Information Resources, Washington DC
11. Guenther R, Dappert A, Peyrard S (2016) An introduction to the PREMIS data dictionary for digital preservation metadata. In: Dappert A, Guenther R, Peyrard S (eds) Digital preservation metadata for practitioners. Springer, Berlin. https://doi.org/10.1007/978-3-319-43763-7_17

PREMIS Advanced Topics

6

6.1 Learning Objectives

The primary goal of this chapter is to extend the use cases for PREMIS by:

- Relating objects in PREMIS
- Employing PREMIS as a data structure to manage version control
- Using PREMIS to track digital provenance

6.2 PREMIS in a Complicated Digital World

From the beginning PREMIS has been designed with a very clear purpose, summarized by a set of principles:

- It is geared toward digital preservation
- It is meant to capture core preservation metadata
- It is technically neutral
- It is domain-agnostic.

–Zierau and Peyrard, 2016 [1]

In the previous chapter, we explored basic functions of PREMIS and its high-level entities. As a core metadata standard that is domain-agnostic, it captures only that information that most institutions need most of the time. As a result, **event** and **agent** entities, which play a supporting role in the provenance of digital objects, have minimal required semantic units. In making a simple PREMIS record for a digital video, we expressed basic technical information such as size and format: in other words, technically neutral metadata. PREMIS

© The Author(s), under exclusive license to Springer Nature Switzerland AG 2022
R. Bettivia et al., *Documenting the Future: Navigating Provenance Metadata Standards*,
Synthesis Lectures on Information Concepts, Retrieval, and Services,
https://doi.org/10.1007/978-3-031-18700-1_6

was designed to work as a digital preservation support system in a variety of environments, from libraries and archives to data science and research collections, regardless of the types of digital content these organizations aim to preserve. Records can be relatively simple, with a minimum set of required semantic units. Additionally, many commercial and open-source tools can automatically generate PREMIS records from basic data entry or technical metadata readouts (Fig. 6.1).

However, PREMIS' flexibility also leaves room for incredible semantic richness. The example in the previous chapter is very object oriented, in a way that fits neatly within PREMIS' data model: there is a preservation target, the sample digital video file, that is the focus of all the linked **object**, **event**, **agent**, and **rights** entities.

Increasingly, however, provenance documentation challenges an object-oriented perspective. The complexity of digital objects in the current landscape often means that digital content itself does not function as neatly bounded objects. At their most basic, digital documents or websites link to other content, requiring a documentalist to determine whether linked content consists of multiple objects or comprises a single, multi-part object. One issue is how much status is given to the links themselves: they are not objects, but they are important to the functionality of the objects that are targets of preservation.

Fig. 6.1 The BitCurator opensource digital forensics environment is one of many platforms, systems, and tools that can generate PREMIS XML records. Lee, C. (2020). Introduction to BitCurator Slide Deck. BitCuratorEdu. https://bitcuratoredu.web.unc.edu/resources/

Digital content like video games or social media provide even more of a challenge to an object-oriented worldview. A social network is not a single thing, but instead is a mnemonic experience that depends on myriad physical, digital and temporal factors such as what device someone uses to access the network; whether one uses an app or a web browser; and news feeds and trends that are populated by algorithms pulling data from content being fed to the network by users all around the world. A single user experience of a social network is very much a butterfly effect situation: if an event happening thousands of miles away changes, so too does the content generated about it, and therefore so too does the user's experience of posts, alerts and advertisements. What does preserving the provenance of social network user experiences look like?

The simple working definition of provenance we anchor this book with is: a *description of how something has come to be*. Answering questions about how to construct and preserve these descriptions depends on the organization doing the provenance labor and which pasts they want to communicate to the future. A company that owns complicated digital content, like a social media or digital advertising company, keeps different software versions on many servers that it combines with user-inputted data, where 'user' includes individuals sharing life updates, companies paying for advertising, influencers laboring in digital spaces, and many others. For collecting institutions, it might mean using an API to pull down JSON content; extracted text and images; or even screengrabs of specific posts, accounts, or trends that match the institution's collecting mandates.

Provenance documentation in these cases requires the creation of artificial boundaries on experiences that occur at the confluence of digital and social interactions in order to make a nebulous interplay of digital experiences into a set of fixed objects. Within the PREMIS data model, this can be expressed as a representation object that is *representedBy* (1.13.2 relationshipSubType) a series of discrete file objects.

Chapters 3 and 4 defined prospective provenance, digital provenance of technological conditions that allows us to document what *will be*. Understanding that provenance can both look back to that past and forward to the future is crucial to developing approaches to documenting digitally mediated social interactions because that flexibility towards potential unfixed outcomes matches the highly context- and temporal-dependent experience of social media engagements: in the case of any social media interaction, there are many other interactions that equally *could have been*. How do we create digital traces to represent this?

6.3 Software Environments in PREMIS

Another challenge when working towards the longevity of digital content, of access or understanding or reuse, is the multitude of dependencies every file has: the conceptual, logical, and physical layers of technology [2]. Files are defined by PREMIS as a "named and ordered sequence of Bytes that is known by an operating system" [3]. But files require software to render them, and that software requires an operating system to run. The operating system requires software libraries, drivers, and hardware. There are many other potential dependencies for digital objects: specialized peripherals like monitors, mouses, or game controllers; sound cards and graphics cards; and even analog components that interact with the software. The components of a functional computing environment for a digital object have dependencies of their own. These dependencies constitute a rhizomatic web of additional content that continues branching outward unless it stops at hardcopy specification documents for programs or schematics and patents for hardware. The applications that support digital content are both essential to digital preservation work and a challenge to digital preservationists because they too are built of 1s and 0s that fall under their care.

Further, while digital objects often have extensive documentation, like standardized signatures and features that appear in file format registries, no such comprehensive registry currently exists for the supporting applications themselves. For example, a search of the PRONOM format registry reveals a wealth of information about several moving image formats, like the one DROID identified in the video file example in Chap. 5. There is comparably less documentation for applications and executable content.

PREMIS, serialized as XML or using the RDF OWL ontology, allows us to document **links** between high-level entities, but also **relationships** between objects. These relationships provide the ability to document the levels of hardware and software needed to render simple content like the sample digital video. They are also the key to documenting the complex webs that represent those *amorphous* digital objects.

The suggested controlled vocabulary for these relationshipTypes (semantic unit 1.13.1) has six options to document the ways in which different objects rely on or relate to each other (Table 6.1). These relationship types support the formalized documentation of digital dependencies. Structural relationships tie a group of **files** to the **representation** that aggregates them. In much the way a FRBR work has many expressions, manifestations, and items, the structural relationship ties together the four types of objects in PREMIS [4]. RelationType such as derivation and replacement touch on digital preservation-specific actions such as emulation and compression.

The *dependency* relationshipType relates digital content to rendering software and hardware. Even when delving into this space of semantic richness, the goal of PREMIS to be

Table 6.1 The type controlled vocabulary for PREMIS, hosted by library of congress. https://id.loc. gov/vocabulary/ preservation/ relationshipType.html

Scheme members
Dependency
Derivation
Logical
Reference
Replacement
Structural

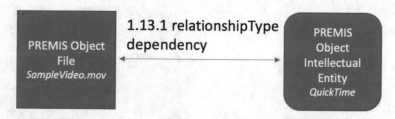

Fig. 6.2 Dependency relationship between two PREMIS objects, a file and a functional rendering software environment

a core metadata standard remains in place. When using PREMIS intellectual entity objects to document software and hardware environments, the aim is not to create a bloated list of every operating system or monitor that will open and render a contemporary .mov file. We make an appraisal about the technological environment we are best able to support in the long term, about which provenance to include. The addition of the PREMIS semantic unit **1.13.6 relatedEnvironmentCharacteristic** can be used to indicate an environment known to work, rather than trying to list all the environments that could possibly work. An environment can be something as simple as a single application. The application, documented as a particular type of intellectual entity designated as an environment, is connected to a file by way of a dependency relationship (Fig. 6.2).

PREMIS also includes a semantic unit, **1.13.2 relationshipSubType**, with its own controlled vocabulary to further specify the nature of the relationship between two objects. Relationships are bidirectional at the discretion of the user: it is possible to express the relationship in both directions, but not necessarily. According to factors like the access and search mechanisms of the system or size and scope of the collection of digital objects, those making the metadata can decide which direction(s) to express in the record (Fig. 6.3).

Environments can also encompass a set of connected intellectual entities. In the example above, QuickTime software could be related to a computer operating system and the hardware on which that operating system runs. The three rendering objects–software, OS, and hardware–connect to each other. The sample video file is related to a software application

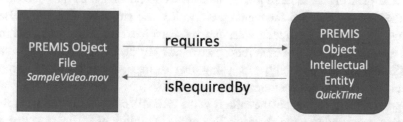

Fig. 6.3 SubType Dependency relationship between two PREMIS objects; SubTypes are directionally specific

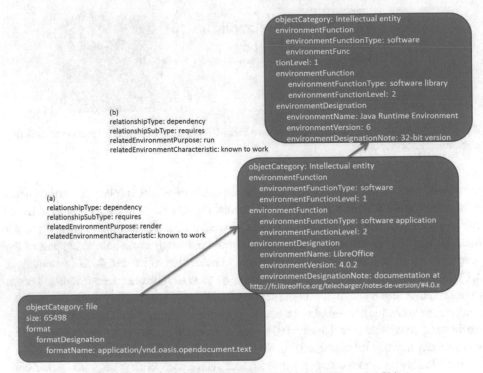

**Figure 4: Dependency relationships between (a) a content and environment Object
and (b) between two environment Objects.**

Fig. 6.4 Figure from the PREMIS Data Dictionary showing a file dependent on software, which is
in turn dependent on a software library

and simultaneously can maintain an association to the other environmental components by
way of their shared relationship to QuickTime (Fig. 6.4).

The relationships in PREMIS enable the documentation of provenance of an intercon-
nected set of objects. It is possible to express the relationships between simple and complex
objects and their digital rendering environments using relationshipTypes and SubTypes.
While PREMIS is designed for digital preservation, the structure of the model enables
provenance expressions for a much wider range of scenarios. In much the way that ProvONE
enables the documentation of both retrospective and prospective provenances, so too can
PREMIS express many possibilities including what has happened and what will happen, via
related objects, events, and customized vocabularies.

The previous chapter laid out the entirety of the PREMIS controlled vocabulary for event
types, from accession to virus checking. Part of the flexibility of PREMIS is that most of
its vocabularies are recommended rather than required. An institution may supplement the

list of existing terms with additional provenance related actions, such as *authentication*, *patching* or *executedSubprogram*.

In the following exercise, we will tackle a common provenance-related challenge, version control. Version control is a provenance issue that represents a challenge in many fields: document versions, software versions, experimental protocol versions all play important roles in understanding information and conducting research. Different OCR software versions might render scanned text differently; different versions of a file format database might label the same file with a different identifier as databases are updated with new information. Versioning impacts user experiences in minor and major ways. The creation of new versions can be ongoing with contemporary digital content; at some juncture, most content will stop updating as its creators stop supporting changes. In the following mini-exercise, we will explore documenting provenance within PREMIS by experimenting with version control.

6.4   Mini-Exercise

'Animal Crossing: New Horizons' debuted for Nintendo Switch in March 2020, right as the United States was heading into its first coronavirus lockdown. The idyllic social simulation game became the console's second-best-selling game yet, helping people around the world connect during an isolating time...–Silberling, 2021 [5]

Chapter 4 introduced the popular Nintendo video game, *Animal Crossing: New Horizons (ACNH)*. *ACNH* is a DIY simulation game in which players can personalize their own virtual islands by making and purchasing tools, furniture, food, and other decor. Nintendo periodically releases updates to *ACNH*, bringing in new features and seasonal items. *ACNH* encapsulates the major and minor experiential disruption caused by software version changes. Periodic updates have added things as minor as football-shaped rugs for the end of the US football post-season (an annual update in February to coincide with the American Football "Super Bowl") to major changes like the ability to swim in the sea and dive for sea creatures that can be sold, eaten, and collected in a museum (Version 1.3.0, released July 2, 2020). In 2021, Nintendo released a large update for *ACNH* and declared that it was done with major developments for the *New Horizons* title of the long-running *Animal Crossing* series. A list of software updates and the game changes they entailed can be found here on Nintendo UK's webpage.[1]

When using PREMIS to document software version changes, start with the basic building blocks, both in terms of the software applications and PREMIS entities. We will begin with the primary targets of PREMIS, the objects. Recall that objects can be intellectual entities, representations, files, and bitstreams. What kinds of objects do you need? For this exercise, it is not necessary to document every version. Rather, we can practice by thinking about

---

[1]   https://www.nintendo.co.uk/Support/Nintendo-Switch/Game-Updates/How-to-Update-Animal-Crossing-New-Horizons-1745568.html.

the main structure of a version. What major entities are involved when a new version is released? What types of objects should be used?

1.1.2 objectIdentifierValue (M, NR)	1.2 objectCategory (M, NR)

Figure 6.5 illustrates a possible combination of objects that begin to construct a version history of a video game, a description of how the most current gaming experience came to be. At the top level, an intellectual entity object encompasses the large, malleable work of the video game title *Animal Crossing: New Horizons*. Each version is a representation object, made up of a series of file objects including the propriety file format for the game software.

Another facet of PREMIS that aids in this versioning process is the **event** entity. The recommended event vocabulary for PREMIS has multiple terms that might be applied to the process of tracking software versions. What terms might you employ to document the

Fig. 6.5 PREMIS objects representing a particular version of a video game that goes through a series of updates over time

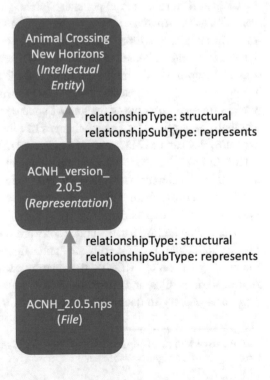

provenance of software versions? Additionally, it is possible to use terms outside the recommended vocabulary. What kinds of terminology not currently in the controlled vocabulary might be useful in documenting software versions? See the full controlled vocabulary for events on the Library of Congress webpage.[2] What other semantic subunits of the event entity might you use to expand on these events to document software versions?

2.2 eventType (M, NR)	Additional event semantic units?

The brevity and non-specificity of the event semantic units is what enables us to create adequate descriptions of a version process. Semantic unit **2.3 eventDateTime** enables us to talk about **when** this update happens. Multiple events with different associated Types and DateTimes mean we can assign multiple dates to the same representation object for ACNH_version_2.0.5. Using the dissemination eventType, defined by Library of Congress as "[t]he process of transmitting or providing access to a copy of the object", we can apply the date of 2022-02-16 to note the date on which the version was released to consumers. The use of modification ("The act of changing a file or bitstream after receipt of the object") describes the receipt of the new game code and subsequent change of experience from the perspective of the user.

The date associated with this modification event might occur on 2022-02-16 or at any point thereafter: it would match the point at which the user actually restarts their game software and acquires the update. We can also employ additional terms outside the existing controlled vocabulary, for example *patching* to describe the release of minor updates to fix bugs and errors, or *moveToProduction* to describe the internal corporate process of packaging the new update and moving it out of the dev environment into the production environment in preparation for the dissemination event. In our example of the 2.0.5 *ACNH* update, these types of events would have happened on dates prior to 2022-02-16.

6.5 Summary

This chapter presents an incremental expansion of usage for the PREMIS provenance standard. It functions as an intellectual exercise for people needing a data structure to document something beyond basic digital preservation, who may want to adapt or move beyond the preservation of static or dynamic yet bounded digital objects. Provenance is a conversation between past, present, and future, expressed by a structured description of how an object

---

[2] https://id.loc.gov/vocabulary/preservation/eventType.html.

came to be. The structures in PREMIS can be employed to formally document workflows that are both retrospective, currently active, and forward-looking, prospective. It moves us towards the ability to document knowledge as process, in much the way PROV and ProvONE document prospective and retrospective provenance, workflows and traces. The next chapter will take on a case study in Nuclear Magnetic Resonance Spectroscopy, where the PREMIS data model is stretched to design and execute workflows for spectral reconstruction.

References

1. Zierau E, Peyrard S (2016) Chapter 14: digital preservation metadata in a metadata ecosystem. In: Dappert A, Squire Guether R, Peyrard S (eds) Digital preservation metadata for practitioners: implementing PREMIS. Springer International, Switzerland
2. Thibodeau K (2002) Overview of technological approaches to digital preservation and challenges in coming years. Council on Library and Information Resources, Washington DC
3. PREMIS Editorial Committee (2015) PREMIS data dictionary for preservation metadata. version 3.0. In: Library of congress. https://www.loc.gov/standards/premis/v3/premis-3-0-final.pdf. Cited 10 Mar 2022
4. Coyle K (2015) FRBR, before and after: a look at our bibliographic models. American Library Association, Chicago
5. Silberling A (2021) Animal crossing: new horizons will get major updates and 'happy home paradise' DCL on November 5. In: TechCrunch. https://techcrunch.com/2021/10/15/animal-crossing-new-horizons-will-get-major-updates-and-happy-home-paradise-dlc-on-november-5/?guccounter=1. Cited 10 Mar 2022

7.1 Learning Objectives

In this chapter we will review provenance capture in the domain of Nuclear Magnetic Resonance Spectroscopy. Using PREMIS as a structure, this chapter will cover:

- Using PREMIS within a Workflow Management System
- PREMIS for both prospective and retrospective provenance
- Embedding a domain-specific language within the PREMIS framework using PREMIS extensions
- Including analytics within a PREMIS record

7.2 Introduction

This book has focused on provenance standards that aim to support the work of a wide variety of domain spaces. In particular, we acknowledge that digital objects and related computational data present new challenges to our traditional understandings of provenance, unmooring them from the past and broadening them to include the present, the future, and the subjunctive conditions (what could have been). The PROV family of standards are designed to support eSciences, to help scientists document their inputs, processes, and output for communication and reproducibility. In this chapter, we consider a specific domain space, Nuclear Magnetic Spectroscopy (NMR).

This scientific community uses sophisticated mathematical algorithms to clean and transform their datasets for subsequent analysis. Traditionally, this data cleaning/transformation has been performed using a pipeline approach where several mathematical operations are chained together to produce an **output** [1]. Until recently, scientists in this domain struggled to document retrospective provenance for these computations. Without a tool to document retrospective provenance, the planned scripts which served to orchestrate the processing (prospective provenance) have stood as proxies for retrospective provenance. Note that this is in stark contrast from examples in earlier chapters where retrospective provenance was used as a guide for prospective. In this community, prospective provenance has been used as a guide for retrospective.

Standards like PROV are designed to assist in the documentation of exactly this kind of provenance work. However, this chapter describes a workflow management system for NMR data processing which records both prospective and retrospective provenance that uses the PREMIS framework, stretching this digital preservation standard into the larger world of provenance documentation [2, 3]. Additionally, this chapter moves beyond theoretical exercises to show how the application of PREMIS as a provenance model works in the real world and what kinds of products and results it generates. Much like the relationship between D-OPM and workflow tools such as Kepler or Taverna or the relationship between PREMIS and digital asset support tools like BitCurator or Preservica, which build and generate provenance records, the workflow management system described in this chapter automatically records the provenance metadata upon execution of the workflow, packaging it with the final output. The examples in this chapter are intended to illustrate provenance in practice, albeit for a specialized domain.

7.3   Nuclear Magnetic Resonance Spectroscopy

First, we will begin with a brief description of this scientific domain. Nuclear Magnetic Resonance (NMR) Spectroscopy is a technique for investigating the biophysical properties of molecules at atomic resolution. NMR exploits the fact that individual nuclei in matter have magnetic moments which can be aligned and perturbed in the presence of a large magnetic field. Some readers might be familiar with the concept of Magnetic Resonance Imaging (MRI): you might have had one when a doctor needed to get an image of something inside your body. If you have had an MRI, you probably remember the many warnings about the strong magnetic fields; an imaging specialist might ask you to remove jewelry before getting near the machine. NMR operates in a similar way, utilizing super-conducting magnets to create and sustain magnetic field strengths of the order of a few Tesla (a measurement unit for magnetic flux density) for MRI and up to 25 Tesla for NMR.[1]

While MRI is used to image tissues and organs, NMR spectroscopy is used to investigate the structure, dynamics, chemistry and mechanism of action of molecules at atomic resolution. Common applications of NMR spectroscopy include determining the three-dimensional structure of proteins and nucleic acids, estimating the relative mobility of portions of macro-

---

[1] The Bruker Corporation announced the availability of the first ever 25.9 Tesla superconducting magnet at the 60th Experimental NMR Conference, April, 2019, Pacific Grove, California, USA. https://www.bruker.com/en/news-and-events/news/2019/bruker-announces-worlds-first-superconducting-1-1-gigahertz-magnet-for-high-resolution-nmr-in-structural-biology.html.

molecules, measuring the binding of drugs to their targets, and screening of metabolites in body fluids as a health diagnostic. In all these applications, the spectroscopist collects data as a trace of oscillations in time and then subsequently converts the data into a frequency plot to study [4].

7.3.1   Spectral Reconstruction

The computational process of converting NMR data from the time domain to the frequency domain is referred to as *spectral reconstruction* (See Fig. 7.1). The simplest method for spectral reconstruction is to apply a Fourier transform (FT) to the data. As NMR signals both decay and oscillate during the data collection, the NMR spectrum after a FT yields a collection of peaks which can be characterized by their intensity (either height or area under the peak are typical metrics for intensity), their resonance frequency (typically reported relative to a reference compound) and their line width at half height (which is related to the decay of the signal in time).

   In practice, spectral reconstruction is far more complicated. First, the datasets are typically multi-dimensional, with one axis being recorded in real time and additional axes recording in virtual time (through repetition of the experiment with variable delays to create the virtual time dimensions). Second, the data points are complex (consisting of two orthogonal readings for each time point). Third, there are multiple mathematical transformations and manipulations applied to the data which are used collectively to remove/replace outliers, reduce noise and other spectral artifacts; and to increase the resolution of the spectra (the ability to distinguish nearby signals). A common spectral reconstruction will apply a few dozen mathematical operations, typically in a pipeline fashion, with a small amount of manual inspection/intervention. There are many software programs which have been designed to aid in the task of spectral reconstruction, some from vendors and others developed by the NMR community at large.

7.3.2   NMRbox

NMRbox is the colloquial name for both the National Center for NMR Data Processing and Analysis as well as the virtual machines hosted and supported by the Center [5]. To put it simply, NMRbox is an Ubuntu operating system image loaded with hundreds of academic software packages useful for processing and/or analyzing NMR data. The NMRbox virtual machine can be downloaded and run on a user's own computer; the Center also hosts cloud-based instances as a Platform as a Service. The online machines are accessed using a Virtual Network Computing (VNC) client which provides a complete desktop experience for a wide assortment of remote devices—from desktops and laptops to tablets and smartphones. As

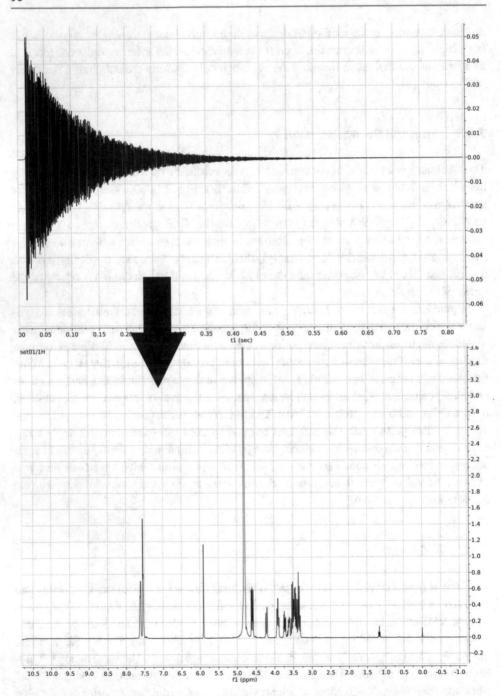

Fig. 7.1 Illustration of spectral reconstruction in which an oscillating signal in time is transformed into a frequency spectrum

part of an agreement with the various software developers whose software is hosted on NMRbox, access to the platform is restricted to academic, not-for-profit use.[2]

The overlapping issues of academically-sourced software with complex dependencies within Linux (Ubuntu) poses many challenges when users want to analyze and publish their data and quickly move on to the next project: users need quick, accessible provenance as an output from their work. Supporting this complex web of software tools and their dependencies is one of the motivations for the NMRbox project.

7.4 CONNJUR

The CONNJUR project predates NMRbox by over a decade. CONNJUR (Connecticut Joint University Research) began in 2002 as an academic collaboration between researchers at the UCONN Health Center, and Rensselaer at Hartford. The goal of CONNJUR is to assist spectroscopists in negotiating the aforementioned web of software tools by providing a software integration environment. The long term vision of CONNJUR is to support the vast majority of available tools which span multiple phases of NMR data processing and analysis [4].

The role of the CONNJUR software integration environment is to tackle the semantic data management issues that spectroscopists are confronted with on a daily basis (file format conversion, for instance) so that these scientists can focus their efforts on the specifics of their research. CONNJUR Spectrum Translator [6] was developed to handle file translation between a myriad of commercial and academically supported software tools. However, in addition to file translation, the various processing tools parameterize their operations in different ways and the semantics of both the individual steps and the process as a whole must also be handled by an integration environment. This was the motivation behind developing the NMR-specific workflow management system called CONNJUR Workflow Builder [2].

7.4.1 CONNJUR Workflow Builder

Throughout this book, we have returned to the importance of being able to adequately describe and document workflows. CONNJUR Workflow Builder is an application for both designing a workflow for spectral reconstruction as well as executing the workflow. As such, recording the provenance of the transformed data is an important feature of the tool. The basic design is to provide a Graphical User Interface (GUI) to allow spectroscopists to create workflows by stitching together nodes called *actors*. The individual steps along the workflow are eventually executed by these actors which typically call a third-party software tool. Workflow Builder handles all of the **parameterization** of the underlying tools as well as

---

[2] The complete terms of use can be found on the NMRbox website (https://nmrbox.org/pages/licensing).

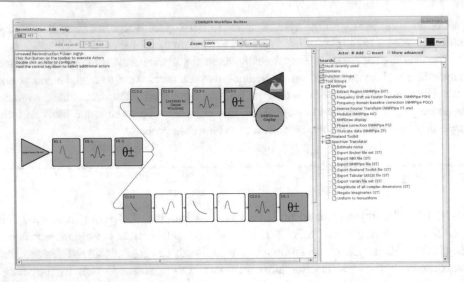

Fig. 7.2 Screenshot of CONNJUR workflow builder

file format conversion between the various file types required by the third-party software tools. Each actor can have its own GUI window to help guide the user in setting proper parameters for the computation, and for helping with terminology by providing translation between the various tools. A screenshot of Workflow Builder is shown in Fig. 7.2.

Question: The "file format" for spectral processing tools is typically a collection of files. One or more files containing the raw data and one or more files containing the metadata. Which PREMIS v 3 object subcategory would you choose to represent NMR data?

Discussion: Some things to consider would be the file types and number of files. Which PREMIS objects aggregates multiple files within a single object? You can compare your decision to Fig. 7.3.

The screenshot in Fig. 7.2 shows the basic canvas on which a workflow is created. The box-shapes are individual **actors** which receive data, apply some mathematical transformation, and then provide the newly transformed data to the next actor in the sequence. The different actors are classified using a few hierarchies (shown in the panel on the right-hand side) based on the type of data accepted (domain), the type of processing done (function groups), and the software tool which handles the processing (tool groups). Each box has either embedded text or a glyph which represents its function (the glyphs are meaningful to the NMR community and are not meant for a general audience). It is worth noting that workflows can easily be forked into multiple branches. For example, in the figure, after the 6th operation, that data is used as input for two separate transformation, one using the upper branch and one using the lower branch.

The boxes are color-coded representing various states of the application.[3] In the figure, pink represents an actor which is configured correctly but has not yet been executed; white represents an actor which is set to be bypassed in the current execution; green represents an actor which has successfully completed; and magenta represents an actor in which additional user input is required to configure the actor for execution. The colors change during an actual execution of a workflow to give a visual cue as to the progress of the reconstruction process. A video showing a workflow execution can be found at metaprov.org.

There are three basic shapes for actors, providing another visual cue. Squares are actors which transform input data into output data (as described above). Circles are actors which are only used for visualizing the data at that node and do not transform the data. Triangles at the beginning or end of a workflow branch are used for importing data into the system or exporting data out of the system. The parameter yet to be set in the magenta triangle is the filename of the exported dataset.

Finally, there are many options we can take for each individual actor icon: we can configure the actor for execution; see a table of metadata defining the properties of the dataset; run a workflow up to that particular actor; and reset an executed workflow back to that actor. We can also show the **provenance** of the dataset up to that point (Fig. 7.3). The provenance recording uses the PREMIS framework along with a NMR-specific model and is encoded using XML.

7.5   PREMIS Meets NMR

The workflow model for CONNJUR Workflow Builder decomposes the workflow into modular processing steps that are conducted by "actors" which operate on datasets. Each actor along the workflow takes data as input, applies some transformation, and outputs the newly transformed data. The transformations done by the actor use calls to the external software tools supported by Workflow Builder.

This model maps conveniently to the PREMIS model. In Chap. 5, we learned that PREMIS supports four, top-level entities: **agents**, **objects**, **events**, and **rights**. The actors map to **events**, when any actor "fires", or completes its task, it results in a transformation of the data. The datasets map to **objects**; in the case of NMR data, the datasets are all digital files. Remember that in PREMIS, agents are typed using a four-item controlled vocabulary: agents can be people, organizations, software, or hardware. Software becomes an agent when it takes on the role of executing an event. The external software tools (as well as CONNJUR itself) are software agents. For the purposes of spectral reconstruction, it is assumed that the scientists own their data and rights management is not support by Workflow Builder. However, it would be possible to assign rights to the datasets if that was deemed important, using PREMIS **rights** entities.

---

[3] The colors are a user preference and can be adjusted or remapped as desired.

Fig. 7.3 Screenshot of the provenance viewer built into Workflow Builder

It is worth recalling the distinction between prospective and retrospective provenance from Chap. 4. Prospective provenance is the concept of a workflow: defining what is intended to be done or what could be done. Retrospective provenance is a recording of what actually happened. In Workflow Builder, those two concepts are separated with different vocabulary: a "workflow" is the prospective version while a "reconstruction" is the retrospective version, the trace.

In the first implementation of Workflow Builder, both workflows and reconstructions were stored using a custom XML schema. Subsequently, PREMIS has been used as the general framework for both workflows and reconstructions [3]. PREMIS provides the top-level entities to record each of the events, agents and objects; while a streamlined, domain-specific schema is used for details of each of these items. Starting with PREMIS v 3.0, each of these three objects has "extension" elements which allow embedding custom schemas within the PREMIS XML document (Fig. 7.4).

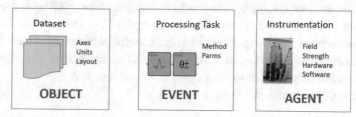

Fig. 7.4 CONNJUR-ML encoded in PREMIS

7.5.1   Agent Extensions

Agents in PREMIS are the people, institutions or organizations, software or hardware which are associated with PREMIS objects. In Workflow Builder, there are three main agents: the *user* who executed the workflow, the *scientific instrument* that collected the data, and the *software tools* that the steps of the workflow. Workflow Builder itself is a software agent that executes the entire workflow and potentially handles a few individual steps.

An example of a software agent linked to a workflow step (event) is shown below:

```
<premis:agent>
 <premis:agentIdentifier>
  <premis:agentIdentifierType>local
</premis:agentIdentifierType>
  <premis:agentIdentifierValue>CONNJUR spectrum
translator</premis:agentIdentifierValue>
 </premis:agentIdentifier>
 <premis:agentName>CONNJUR spectrum
translator</premis:agentName>
 <premis:agentType>software</premis:agentType>
 <premis:linkingEventIdentifier>
  <premis:linkingEventIdentifierType>local
</premis:linkingEventIdentifierType>
  <premis:linkingEventIdentifierValue>Event-000
</premis:linkingEventIdentifierValue>
 </premis:linkingEventIdentifier>
</premis:agent>
```

In the context of agent extensions (PREMIS semantic unit 3.6 agentExtension), the agent that requires customized metadata is the scientific instrument. In NMR spectroscopy, spectroscopists need to know what the overall field strength of the spectrometer is, as well as aspects of which nuclei can be perturbed along each dimension of a multi-dimensional experiment. The PREMIS agentExtension is used to add this customization to the *spectrometer agent*, which is linked to the first *dataset object* in the workflow.

An example of this is shown below:

```
<premis:agent>
 <premis:agentIdentifier>
  <premis:agentIdentifierType>local
</premis:agentIdentifierType>
  <premis:agentIdentifierValue>SP-001
</premis:agentIdentifierValue>
 </premis:agentIdentifier>
 <premis:agentName>UCONN Health Varian 600
<\/premis:agentName>
 <premis:agentType>hardware</premis:agentType>
 <premis:agentExtension>
  <connjur:spectrometer>
   <connjur:strength units="T">14.1</connjur:strength>
   <connjur:channel>
    <connjur:nucleus>1H</connjur:nucleus>
    <connjur:frequency units="Mhz">599.98</connjur:frequency>
   </connjur:channel>
   <connjur:channel>
    <connjur:nucleus>13C</connjur:nucleus>
    <connjur:frequency units="Mhz">150.54</connjur:frequency>
   </connjur:channel>
   <connjur:channel>
    <connjur:nucleus>15N</connjur:nucleus>
    <connjur:frequency units="Mhz">60.78</connjur:frequency>
   </connjur:channel>
  </connjur:spectrometer>
 </premis:agentExtension>
 </premis:agent>
```

7.5.2 Event Extensions

Events in a workflow represent the various processing steps which occur along the way. In Workflow Builder, these events are handled by actors which are parameterized to fine tune their action. In the context of the retrospective provenance of a scientific processing workflow, knowing the precise configuration of these processing steps (events) is paramount. The events are bidirectionally linked to the digital objects which act as input and/or output to the event. Below is an example illustrating how Workflow Builder uses PREMIS to document a processing step which is implemented through the tool NMRpipe [1].

```
<premis:event>
 <premis:eventIdentifier>
  <premis:eventIdentifierType>local
</premis:eventIdentifierType>
  <premis:eventIdentifierValue>Event-004
</premis:eventIdentifierValue>
 </premis:eventIdentifier>
 <premis:eventType>nmrPipe -fn FT</premis:eventType>
 <premis:eventDateTime>Wed Sep 05 13:52:44 EDT
2018</premis:eventDateTime>
 <premis:eventDetailInformation>
  <premis:eventDetailExtension>
   <connjur:configuration
xmlns:connjur="https://.../connjur-ml.xsd">
   <connjur:setAutomatically>true
</connjur:setAutomatically>
   <connjur:negateImaginaries>false
</connjur:negateImaginaries>
   <connjur:dimension>1</connjur:dimension>
  </connjur:configuration>
  </premis:eventDetailExtension>
 </premis:eventDetailInformation>
</premis:event>
```

The eventDetailExtension (2.4.2 eventDetailExtension) semantic unit is used for custom XML which provides additional, relevant information for spectroscopists. One important item is which dimension (*connjur:dimension*) the event relates to. This dimension is further linked to the hardware through the agent metadata of the previous section.

7.5.3   Object Extensions

In Workflow Builder, the PREMIS *object* refers to the scientific datasets which are produced after each processing step, and which in turn are consumed by the next processing step. In NMR spectroscopy, the file formats tend to be collections of files in which the numeric data is in one or more files and the textual metadata in another. For that reason, the PREMIS object in the following example is of type *representation*, the PREMIS object type that allows us to group a set of files that together comprise a single entity. In some configurations of the workflow execution, a single file is piped from one actor to another. In that case, the PREMIS object would be a file object.

```xml
<premis:object xsi:type="premis:representation">
 <premis:objectIdentifier>
  <premis:objectIdentifierType>local
</premis:objectIdentifierType>
  <premis:objectIdentifierValue>13C,15N
HSQC-000</premis:objectIdentifierValue>
 </premis:objectIdentifier>
 <premis:significantProperties>
 <premis:significantPropertiesType>format<
/premis:significantPropertiesType>
 <premis:significantPropertiesValue>varian
</premis:significantPropertiesValue>
  <premis:significantPropertiesExtension>
   <connjur:spectrum
xmlns:connjur="https://...connjur-ml.xsd">
    <connjur:spectrumIdentifier>13C,15N
HSQC-00</connjur:spectrumIdentifier>
    <connjur:spectralDimensions>2
</connjur:spectralDimensions>
    <connjur:spectralAxis>
     <connjur:decoupledNucleus>H1
</connjur:decoupledNucleus>
     <connjur:domain>time</connjur:domain>
     <connjur:sweepwidth units="Hz">8511
</connjur:sweepwidth>
     <connjur:spectralFrequency
units="MHz">600</connjur:spectralFrequency>
     <connjur:pointType>complex</connjur:pointType>
```

```
        <connjur:totalPoints>1024</connjur:totalPoints>
        <connjur:negateImaginaries>true
    </connjur:negateImaginaries>
        <connjur:constantPhase>051</connjur:constantPhase>
        <connjur:linearPhase>000</connjur:linearPhase>
        <connjur:sampling>uniform</connjur:sampling>
      </connjur:spectralAxis>
     <connjur:spectralAxis>
        <connjur:decoupledNucleus>C13
    </connjur:decoupledNucleus>
        <connjur:domain>time</connjur:domain>
        <connjur:sweepwidth units="Hz">3000
    </connjur:sweepwidth>
        <connjur:spectralFrequency
    units="MHz">151</connjur:spectralFrequency>
        <connjur:pointType>complex</connjur:pointType>
        <connjur:totalPoints>128</connjur:totalPoints>
        <connjur:negateImaginaries>true
    </connjur:negateImaginaries>
        <connjur:constantPhase>001</connjur:constantPhase>
        <connjur:linearPhase>000</connjur:linearPhase>
        <connjur:sampling>uniform</connjur:sampling>
       </connjur:spectralAxis>
     </connjur:spectrum>
    </premis:significantPropertiesExtension>
   </premis:significantProperties>
  </premis:object>
```

In this example, Workflow Builder uses the *significantPropertiesExtension* (1.4.3 significantPropertiesExtension) to embed the custom metadata. In future releases, this will be changed to the *objectCharacteristicsExtension* semantic unit (1.5.7 objectCharacteristicsExtension), because significant properties hold a special meaning to the digital preservation community that doesn't comport well with this particular usage.

It is in this custom metadata where the spectrometer channels which were described in the agent are formally mapped to the object characteristics which provide the context for the event parameterization. The object characteristics are clearly the most detailed extensions including many metadata fields which give context to the NMR spectral dataset being processed. As the next section will describe, this metadata can include metrics regarding data quality and other properties of these intermediate datasets.

7.6   Analytics

A recent addition to Workflow Builder is the ability to record metrics of the intermediate datasets as they are created throughout the workflow [7]. As mentioned earlier, spectral reconstruction uses a fairly complicated workflow approach in order to improve data quality (sensitivity, resolution, etc.). Part of the provenance description is tracking how these spectral properties change throughout the processing workflow. While NMR datasets are not excessively large, they are big enough that a spectroscopist is not inclined to store each intermediate created. For that reason, CONNJUR Workflow Builder has been adapted to calculate metrics on data quality at each step along the workflow. The intermediate datasets themselves are deleted, but the metrics are stored within the PREMIS record as part of the **object's** significant properties (1.4 significantProperties). Packaging these analytics in with the rest of the PREMIS provenance record makes them accessible to anyone interested in the reconstructed spectrum. This transforms a simple dataset into a research object.

7.7   Summary

In this chapter, we introduced a real-world example of PREMIS' provenance modelling in the real-world. While there are millions of PREMIS records in use in traditional digital preservation settings, Workflow Builder stretches PREMIS beyond the preservation domain space. This chapter covered:

- An introduction to the NMR spectroscopy domain and some provenance needs of the domain
- How PREMIS can be used to document both retrospective and prospective provenance
- How this hybrid provenance becomes its own research object

This latter point is important: at this juncture, provenance moves beyond metadata. The provenance documentation becomes its own primary object of study, its own research subject.

This chapter also teased out some additional nuances in the PREMIS data dictionary. The extension semantic units are used to incorporate custom XML related to NMR spectroscopy. Such extension semantic units can be used in a similar way in many disciplinary or industry spaces, as containers for specific and granular information that exists outside the provenance model. In working with Workflow Builder, we also explored additional object-related semantic units, such as significant properties and object properties beyond those we used in Chap. 5.

References

1. Delaglio F, Grzesiek S, Vuister G, Zhu G, Pfeifer J, Bax A (1995) NMRPipe: a multidimensional spectral processing system based on UNIX pipes. J Biomol NMR 6:277–293
2. Fenwick M, Weatherby G, Vyas J, Sesanker C, Martyn T, Ellis H, Gryk M (2015) CONNJUR Workflow Builder: a software integration environment for spectral reconstruction. J Biomol NMR 62:313–326
3. Heintz D, Gryk M (2018) Curating scientific workflows for biomolecular nuclear magnetic resonance spectroscopy. Int J Digit Curation 13:286
4. Ellis H, Fox-Erlich S, Martyn T, Gryk M (2006) Development of an integrated framework for protein structure determinations: a logical data model for NMR data analysis. In: Third international conference on information technology: new generations (ITNG'06), pp 613–618
5. Maciejewski M, Schuyler A, Gryk M, Moraru I, Romero P, Ulrich E, Eghbalnia H, Livny M, Delaglio F, Hoch J (2017) NMRbox: a resource for biomolecular NMR computation. Biophys J 112:1529–1534
6. Nowling R, Vyas J, Weatherby G, Fenwick M, Ellis H, Gryk M (2011) CONNJUR spectrum translator: an open source application for reformatting NMR spectral data. J Biomol NMR 50:83–89
7. Weatherby G, Gryk MR (2020) CONNJUR Workflow Builder: a software integration environment for spectral reconstruction. Int J Digit Curation. https://doi.org/10.2218/ijdc.v15i1.709

More Provenance, More Problems

8

8.1   Provenance, Then and Now

We began this book with a look at a very traditional set of provenance stories. While full of unexpected twists and turns, the histories of artworks are typical representations of retrospective provenance: reconstructing the story of how an artwork came to be in existence and how it came to be where it currently is today. These types of descriptions are functionally persuasive essays: they communicate a vision into the present and future that must convince recipients of the veracity and authenticity of the objects in question. Even the most ironclad set of data points might fail to convince audiences. Furthermore, the conversation is ongoing: a provenance story that convinces one group of people at one point may not convince a different audience at a different point in time. BBC's *Fake or Fortune* television show explored the case of some Turner-attributed paintings at the National Museum of Wales that have been authenticated and unauthenticated numerous times. These authentication snafus have occurred while the collection has been in the hands of the same museum. This means that the data points that make up the provenance story haven't changed: it is the way the story is received that has.

We have used a simple definition for provenance throughout this text: provenance is a description of how something has come to be. We acknowledge that the simplicity of this definition glosses over the challenging nuances of provenance, especially provenance fulfilling some kind of role in the real world. The art examples highlight some of these important nuances. First, they demonstrate that provenance is not necessarily inherent to an object, or a process, or an agent. Good provenance work is a combination of factors, the right combination for a particular context. Second, provenance mediates a conversation over time. We have called this book *Documenting the Future*, because the story bounces back and forth between retrospective traces of the past and prospective visions of the future, and our documentary practices are as much about reconstructing history as they are about our

© The Author(s), under exclusive license to Springer Nature Switzerland AG 2022
R. Bettivia et al., *Documenting the Future: Navigating Provenance Metadata Standards*,
Synthesis Lectures on Information Concepts, Retrieval, and Services,
https://doi.org/10.1007/978-3-031-18700-1_8

anticipations: anticipating future data functions, future research needs, and future cultural valuations. As the Turner case shows, the conversation moves back in time because our perspectives on what the past looks like change according to our present context. What we document now will change how we see the past and how we will act in times to come.

Pragmatically, this book has taken us on a journey through a selected few standards aimed at structuring descriptions of how things come to be, provenance. We covered PROV and some of its *PROVlets*: derivative standards and extensions designed to expand and improve the granularity of provenance descriptions, designed for computational data and eScience. We also looked at the digital preservation standard PREMIS as a provenance standard, examining how it works cleanly in its own domain and how its flexible structure enables it to do much more than document preservation decisions. We concluded the journey with an in-depth example, moving provenance beyond vignettes and simple examples to a complicated, real-world situation: NMR spectroscopy. In the NMR case study, PREMIS is stretched to new tasks and domains: importantly, PREMIS didn't break in this transformation, but instead rose to the challenge to enable scientists in NMR spectroscopy to bridge the space between prospective and retrospective provenance, documenting algorithmic and computational steps that were taken, that could be taken, and that should be taken.

8.2   PROV in the World

The NMR spectroscopy case study is not an isolated one. The standards covered in this text have found a wide variety of uses in real-world applications. In Chaps. 2, 3, and 4, we illustrate the important elements and attributes for PROV and ProvONE, two standards in a larger family of standards dedicated to documenting computational processes predominantly in eSciences. But the *JeMiRi Winery* example, *Animal Crossing: New Horizons* example, and other examples demonstrated in Chaps. 2 through 4 show that PROV and ProvONE can be used as much in other domains as they can in the eSciences.

As a recap, PROV and ProvONE introduced a wide range of concepts, including:

- Agent
- Activity
- Entity
- Data
- User
- Execution
- Program
- Workflow

PROV and the PROVlets serve as primary stepping stones for conceptual modeling purposes: people use them as reference models on which they can build best practices and recommendations, tools, and workflow systems. For instance, Thessen et al, in discussing curation and metadata best practices for biodiversity data, advocate the use of PROV core components for annotating digital artifacts [1]. McPhillips et al developed the *YesWorkflow* programming script annotation tool based on the concept of *hybrid provenance* [2]. In their work on a genomics workflow, Gaignard, Skaf-Molli, and Belhajjame stressed the importance of intermediate data products within workflow systems, very similar to how ProvONE emphasizes the inputs and outputs of the *data structure* [3]. Prabhune et al directly implemented the ProvONE model in designing their image processing workflow for medical datasets [4].

Moreau and Groth enumerate PROV and PROVlet-related data management tools such as ProvToolBox,[1] ProvPy,[2] ProvValidator,[3] and others [5]. On the W3C PROV Implementation Report [6], there are 66 different PROV implementations extending across application frameworks, APIs, services, vocabulary extensions, and vocabulary usage. However, like data and many other things on the web, implementations of PROV and PROVlets are often ephemeral. Many of the tools listed in the W3C report were last maintained 5–10 years ago (e.g. prov-gen,[4] raw2ld[5]), now defunct (e.g. PROVoKing, CollabMap), or have switched to another service entirely (e.g. StatJR eBook System[6]).

8.3 PREMIS in the World

PREMIS is in widespread use across the world as the current *de facto* standard for digital preservation metadata. PREMIS is built into content management systems,[7] repository systems,[8] and numerous tools (see the BitCurator example in Chap. 6). Dapper, Guenther, and Peyrard's 2016 book [7], *Digital Preservation Metadata for Practitioners*, coincided with the release of the most recent version of PREMIS, version 3.0. In addition to laying out the rationale for PREMIS' semantic units and the functionality of its data model, the book also features a number of real-world case studies. These studies from practitioners take up topics including PREMIS for web archiving work; e-journal preservation; digital forensics and disk image applications; and archives. The book includes a chapter from Phillips and Alemneh on the development of "The PREMIS Event Service" at the University of North Texas Libraries,[9] making PREMIS events searchable, effectively creating a tool that helps users to standardize and explore provenance [8].

---

[1] ProvToolBox:https://github.com/lucmoreau/ProvToolbox.

[2] ProvPy: https://pypi.python.org/pypi/prov.

[3] ProvValidator: https://provenance.ecs.soton.ac.uk/validator/.

[4] prov-gen: https://github.com/PaoloMissier/ProvToolbox/tree/master/prov-gen.

[5] raw2ld: https://github.com/Data2Semantics/raw2ld.

[6] StatJR: https://www.bristol.ac.uk/cmm/software/statjr/index.html

[7] https://www.archivematica.org/en/docs/archivematica-1.4/user-manual/metadata/premis/.

[8] https://wiki.lyrasis.org/display/DSDOC/All+Documentation.

[9] https://premis-event-service.readthedocs.io/en/latest/overview.html.

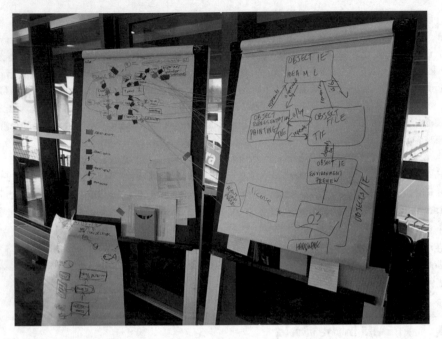

Fig. 8.1 Photo of workshop activity at IDCC 2020, Dublin Ireland

The authors began this project with a series of workshops at conferences like the International Digital Curation Conference (IDCC) and iConference, where we presented a practical introduction to PREMIS, PROV, and ProvONE for a wide variety of users: participants ranged from graduate students to practitioners at state and private archives and universities. A common refrain from participants was the desire to get a handle on provenance issues at their own organizations (Fig. 8.1).

Many of the hands-on activities at these workshops focused on having participants make informal records and create crosswalks between PREMIS and PROV. In pre-pandemic times, participants would literally tie the models together with colored string to show which aspects of each model comported well with related aspects in another. Others have engaged in this kind of labor in practical settings: Li and Sugimoto [9] explored combining PREMIS and PROV to make a model for documenting the provenance of the metadata itself, making the preservation metadata into the target object [9]. This is crucial, as studies like Hart and deVries' [10] demonstrate the vulnerability of digital object metadata. Well-maintained metadata for digital objects like photographs and videos have taken on critical new roles in the current landscape of widespread disinformation campaigns [10].

8.4   Lingering Issues

The nuances and complexities of provenance are compounded by the fact that it is used in so many different domains for so many different projects. It would never be possible to explore all these challenges in a single volume, but we hope we have elucidated some helpful models and made a compelling case for the need to understand the full temporal spectrum of provenance, to understand how it echoes across time. In the remaining sections of this book, we'll bring up a select handful of additional considerations that we believe are promising avenues for future research.

8.4.1   Appraisal

Provenance is frequently employed in relation to appraisal. In the art and archival realms, the appraisal of a work is based in part on the persuasiveness of the related provenance story. The Society of American Archivists defines appraisal as[10]:

- the process of identifying materials offered to an archives that have sufficient value to be accessioned
- the process of determining the length of time records should be retained, based on legal requirements and on their current and potential usefulness
- the process of determining the market value of an item; monetary appraisal

Provenance descriptions play a role especially in the first and third definitions: they help to identify objects and that identity impacts the market value of the objects. The second definition speaks to the need to make a determination about what records to retain, for how long, and in what form.

In the PROV and the PREMIS chapters, we discuss the need to build provenance documentation carefully. This means not only ensuring you don't leave something important out, it also means selecting what to include judiciously. Rather than recording all possible provenance, it is worth appraising what provenance is necessary for the given context. PREMIS provides a scaffold for recording the most commonly required provenance: the endemic semantic units are designed for core metadata. PREMIS includes extensions so that users can document additional information they deem important, what they appraise as necessary for their particular circumstances. In Chap. 7, Workflow Builder puts customized XML into these extensions to provide information specific to NMR data.

Appraisal is not a one-off event: it's an on-going process. Content stewards constantly reapply appraisal criteria to items in a collection. This process relates to the record scheduling

---

[10] https://dictionary.archivists.org/entry/appraisal.html.

described in the second SAA definition for appraisal. It is also echoed in data cycle models, like the Digital Curation Centre (DCC) data curation life cycle.[11] In the DCC model, appraisal and reappraisal appear as prominent steps in a cycle: they must happen again and again. The DCC model refers to 'data', but we argue here that this same approach should be applied to metadata. An avenue for future work would be to examine a "provenance life cycle": how we select, appraise, and reappraise the data points on which we build our provenance stories, and how we tell and retell those stories over time.

8.4.2   Circularity, On Purpose and In Practice

PROV and its PROVlets aim to be reference-level standards. This level of abstraction means they must be many things to many people. As such, we intentionally both simplify and clarify PROV and ProvONE content for this book. The simplification enables us to provide a gentle introduction to the complexity of PROV and the PROVlets. Clarification becomes necessary when reference models move from the realm of the theoretical into practical application. Here, we will look at a representative example. One of the spaces of general agreement between the models we have covered in this book is the similarity between some of the top-level entities in each one. Agent is one such entity, one that occurs in PROV and PREMIS. The concept of agency and the different types of humans and machines that occupy these roles are essential in telling provenance stories.

Upon close examination, **agent** in PROV is a more challenging term than what one might immediately expect from the class diagram in the W3C documentation [11, 12]. Entities are disjoint from activities. As we learned in Chap. 3, agents can be either **entities** or **activities**. Essentially, agents are either an entity or an activity which stands in a specialized role. That allows one to create a completely valid provenance graph in Python Prov (Fig. 8.2).

Our super smart co-author Michael Gryk has created a PROV model instance to demonstrate the process of how someone learns about something. This kind of provenance concern, how we know what we know, is a widely explored one that even has models of its own. One example is the CIDOC-CRM extension CRMInf which is designed to model inferences and allow people to explain how they know what they know when dealing with primary sources.[12] This example demonstrates the complexity of using consistent symbols when diagramming with PROV. In this instance, *textbook* and *smart_michael* are entities. *Study* is an activity. *ignorant_michael* is an entity in its usage by study and the derivation of *smart_michael*. However, *ignorant_michael* is also an **agent** who was associated with the activity of studying using the *textbook* **entity**. *ignorant_michael* is also an **agent** attributed to the **entity** *smart_michael*. This leads to a kind of circularity in the use of agents in PROV. This circularity brings to mind the famous M.C. Escher lithograph, *Drawing Hands* (Fig. 8.3): the agents are mutually constitutive in a way that works in a model or a piece of art-

---

[11] DCC curation lifecycle model: https://www.dcc.ac.uk/guidance/curation-lifecycle-model.

[12] https://cidoc-crm.org/crminf/.

Fig. 8.2 PROV-ing the studying and learning process

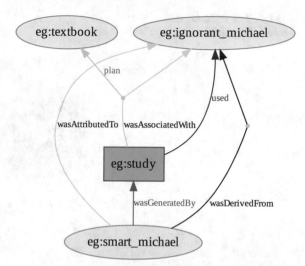

Fig. 8.3 "Drawing Hands" ©2022 The M.C. Escher Company-The Netherlands. All rights reserved. www. mcescher.com

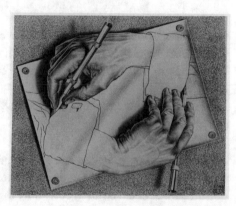

work but that ceases to make sense in the real world. Real world settings also necessarily involve a temporal component that is not as often reproduced, or reproducible, in a model. The *Drawing Hands* illustrates one of the challenges in documenting time: it is impossible to tell from the lithograph which hand came first, which hand is documenting the past and which is documenting contemporaneity or futurity.

PREMIS, unlike PROV, does not use color- and shape-coded diagramming conventions. The agent concept in PREMIS invokes a different kind of circularity, one that was intentional and assumed in the domain space of digital preservation. In digital preservation, practitioners know that tools like software *agents* and software environment *objects* will themselves eventually become targets of preservation, largely as a function of technological change over time. While we might use DROID (Chap. 2) now to help us generate checksums and identify file types, in the future, we might need to preserve the executable code that makes up DROID. Digital preservation embraces this circularity, reminiscent of the on-

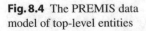

Fig. 8.4 The PREMIS data
model of top-level entities

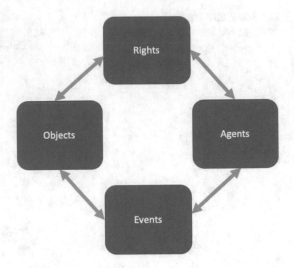

going preservation tasks in the DCC life cycle model we mentioned in Sect. 8.4.1. One way
that PREMIS avoids some of the complexity surrounding the ever changing roles of agents,
both human and machine, is by creating a data structure wherein agents never link directly
to objects (Fig. 8.4).

A single software program, Software X, can be described by three different top-level
entities in PREMIS:

- Software X could be a file or representation **object**
- Software X could be an environment intellectual entity **object**
- Software X could be an **agent**, with 3.3 agentType *software*

Because agents in PREMIS are only connected to objects via events, even if Software X
was documented multiple times within a single XML record, Software X the agent would
not accidentally end up preserving itself, Software X the file object. That kind of relationship
could only happen via mutual, but explicit and intentional, links to an event.

What this does mean is that Software X can be repeated multiple times within a single PREMIS instance—as the representation or file object, the intellectual entity software
environment object, and an agent. One question that arises here is how best to express relationships between those three versions of Software X. All three represent the same set of 1s
and 0s, but what makes them discrete entities is the role they play at a particular moment in
time. It is fair to say that the software that is being preserved is distinct from the software
doing the preserving, even if bytewise they are the same sequence. It is worth remembering
that even when making records of real situations, there is a difference between things as
they are actually in use in the real world and the versions of them that appear in models.
The temporal quality to the distinction between the various versions of Software X, like the

ambiguity of the *Drawing Hands*, is reminiscent of the changeable nature of provenance descriptions. The need for best practices in documenting this changeability is necessary moving forward, particularly in cases like large scale software and application preservation and emulation services.

8.4.3 Cross the Walk with Caution

In metadata practice, the term crosswalking refers to the practice of mapping one standard to another. Crosswalks are one of the most commonly used methods in mapping different metadata standards [13]. It can be a tricky process, with some terms missing data sources or target fields, with one:many and many:one mismatches. Additionally, there are the semantic challenges where even the same word can have vastly different meanings, depending on the context: title in one standard might mean the title of a book, *Documenting the Future*, while title in another standard might refer to someone's professional designation, *Dr.* Yi-Yun Cheng. Likewise, different words that are supposedly synonymous in a crosswalk might be near synonyms, or have subtle differences in meanings. Are *authors* and *creators* the same? What about *authors* and *contributors*?

The standards we have introduced in this book exemplify these challenges: consider the difference between the special concept of agent in PROV and the way agents are used in PREMIS. We see similar challenges when we walk these models from theory to practice. When stretching PREMIS from digital preservation to NMR spectroscopy, researchers decided to shift away from significant properties (1.4.3 significantPropertiesExtension) to object properties (1.5.7 objectCharacteristicsExtension) when embedding custom NMR metadata into records. This decision was made because of the loaded meaning the term *significant properties* carries in the domain of digital preservation. Significant properties have been a persistent challenge in digital preservation. The PREMIS data dictionary provides this information on 1.4 significantProperties [14]:

- **Definition**: Characteristics of a particular object subjectively determined to be important to maintain through preservation actions.
- **Rationale**: Objects that have the same technical properties may still differ as to the properties that should be preserved for future presentation or use.

The role of significant properties is one that bears heavily on provenance, especially when dealing with digital content. This is because long-term access to digital objects often assumes that aspects of the logical object will change over time: the screen on which you view something goes from CRT to LED, the peripheral device goes from wired d-pads to wireless motion controls, operating systems change from Windows to Mac. Significant properties are meant to encapsulate what cannot change about objects over time if they are to maintain sufficient recognizability and authority. Determining what constitutes a significant property and standardizing the process of identifying and documenting them are important on-going challenges in the field of digital preservation.

Determining whether an object maintains its authenticity over time requires documentation of past changes, or retrospective provenance. It also requires intentional approaches to future changes, prospective provenance, and attention to the trickier, more ambiguous, *possible* changes, or **subjunctive provenance**. How much change can happen before the story breaks and becomes two stories, before the provenance of a single object over time becomes the provenance of one object and the provenance of a new, different object? While this concept continues to be a contested space of exploration in digital preservation [15, 16]; there is a research gap that can be filled by bringing significant properties discourse into conversation with provenance.

Finally, there is room for future work on actual crosswalks between existing provenance models. The proliferation of schemas is a common joke in the domain of metadata: nobody wants to use someone else's toothbrush. The implication is that, when identifying challenges or shortcoming of existing schemas, there is a tendency to write a new one, which inevitably introduces new challenges and new shortcomings. This iterative process is part and parcel of working in the real world.

Standards like PROV, the PROVlets, and PREMIS are references at the end of the day. In much the same way that there exists a necessary valley between the description of word meanings in a dictionary and the quotidian uses of those words in real life, there is always a space between the imaginary form of a provenance model and how it gets deployed in practice.

Deploying PROV and PREMIS is both beneficial in some circumstances and challenging, or even untenable, in others. Some organizations might use a model incorrectly on purpose because that better suits their needs; other organizations might choose to avoid a standard altogether, because the barriers to entry are too high or because the affordances are too costly. Rather than contributing to the proliferation of new standards, one option to create best practices in provenance documentation is to create application profiles by combining existing models and borrowing the best bits from each model according to the particular situation.

Luckily, structural features like PREMIS' OWL ontology and namespacing mean this is entirely possible. A critical first step to such work would be an analysis of terminology across standards, such as PROV, the PROVlets, and PREMIS, and potentially additional provenance-oriented standards from other domains, such as the CRMInf reasoning model mentioned in Sect. 8.4.2. This analysis might include a mapping to indicate which terms are unique from standard to standard and where there are overlaps. The topics covered in this book highlight lingering provenance issues that can help to shape a comprehensive inquiry into the current landscape of provenance models.

8.5 Conclusion and a Call for Action

We hope by now we've convinced you that provenance metadata is needed for mirroring both the past and the future. The million dollar question that is probably still lingering in your head, as many of our workshop participants shared, is **what's next**? How do I implement provenance standards in my work? How do I incorporate provenance metadata along with other relevant documentation I have? Are there existing tools I can use to document provenance? The list of million-dollar questions goes on.

There is no one straight-forward answer, because it depends on **you**: how you perceive provenance and the contexts in which you would like to organize provenance data. As much as we value the provenance standards discussed in this book at this point in time, it is important to acknowledge there may be new provenance standards or new PROVlets that surpass PREMIS, PROV, and ProvONE. We thus want to place more emphasis on the motivations and goals behind these models, namely:

- Provenance is fluid and transcends time;
- Creating provenance descriptions is both a conceptual modeling and metadata recording exercise;
- Provenance work is an exercise in persuasion;
- Working with provenance is both a ubiquitous and field-agnostic act.

Throughout this book, we have defined provenance as a description of how something comes to be. Whether you are thinking about adopting provenance models as a museum curator, digital preservationist, climatologist, or data journalist, we hope this book brings out the incentives to make provenance a value-added part of your work and provides a useful dictionary with which you can begin to write your own provenance stories to document your own future.

References

1. Thessen A, Woodburn M, Koureas D, Paul D, Conlon M, Shorthouse D, Ramdeen S (2019) Proper attribution for curation and maintenance of research collections: metadata recommendations of the RDA/TDWG Working Group. Data Sci J 18
2. McPhillips T et al (2015) YesWorkflow: a user-oriented, language-independent tool for recovering workflow information from scripts. Int J Digit Curation 10:298–313
3. Gaignard A, Skaf-Molli H, Belhajjame K (2020) Findable and reusable workflow data products: a genomic workflow case study. Semant Web 11:751–763
4. Prabhune A, Stotzka R, Gertz M, Zheng L, Hesser J (2017) Managing provenance for medical datasets. In: HealthInf 2017: proceedings Of The 10th international conference on health informatics
5. Moreau L, Groth P (2013) Provenance: an introduction to PROV. Synth Lect Semant Web: Theory Technol 3:1–129

6. Huynh TD, Groth P, Zednik S, The W3C PROV implementation report. W3C
7. Dappert A, Guenther R, Peyrard S (2016) Digital preservation metadata for practitioners. Springer, Berlin. https://doi.org/10.1007/978-3-319-43763-7_17
8. Phillips ME, Alemneh DG (2016) Case study: implementing an open-source and in-house developed premis events and agents system. In: Dappert A, Guenther R, Peyrard S (eds) Digital preservation metadata for practitioners. Springer, Berlin. https://doi.org/10.1007/978-3-319-43763-7_17
9. Li C, Sugimoto S (2014) Provenance description of metadata using PROV with PREMIS for long-term use of metadata. In: Proceedings of the DCMI international conference on dublin core and metadata applications. Dublin Core Metadata Initiative, pp 147–156
10. Hart TR, De Vries D (2017) Metadata provenance and vulnerability. Inf Technol Libr 36(4):24–33
11. Moreau L, Groth P, Cheney J, Lebo T, Miles S (2015) The rationale of PROV. J Web Semant 35:235–257
12. Groth P, Moreau L (2013) PROV-overview: an overview of the PROV family of documents. https://www.w3.org/TR/prov-overview/. Cited 10 Mar 2022
13. Chan L, Zeng ML (2006) Metadata interoperability and standardization—a study of methodology part I. D-Lib Mag 12(6):1082–9873
14. PREMIS Editorial Committee (2015) PREMIS data dictionary for preservation metadata. version 3.0. In: Library of congress. https://www.loc.gov/standards/premis/v3/premis-3-0-final.pdf. Cited 10 Mar 2022
15. Hedstrom M, Lee CA (2002) Significant properties of digital objects: definitions, applications, implications. In: Proceedings of the DLM-forum. European Commission, pp 218–223
16. McDonough J, Olendorf R, Kirschenbaum M, Kraus K, Reside D, Donahue R, Phelps A et al (2010) Preserving virtual worlds final report. http://hdl.handle.net/2142/17097. Cited 10 Mar 2022